A Reproduction in Facsimile of

HAMLET

from the

First Folio of 1623

Introduction by

Charles Adams Kelly

2nd Edition

The Triple Anvil Press

at Mystery Ridge

Ann Arbor

Howland Research, LLC
807 Asa Gray Drive
University Commons # 304
Ann Arbor, MI 48105

Kelly, Charles Adams.
    A reproduction in facsimile of Hamlet from the first folio of 1623 – 2nd
Edition / Introduction by Charles Adams Kelly.
    p. cm.
2nd edition.
ISBN 9780966212679

    1. Shakespeare, William, 1564-1616. Hamlet. 2. Shakespeare, William,
1564-1616--Bibliography--Folios. 1623. I. Title.

PR2807 .K41 2008
822.33--dc22   2009931130

Produced by
The Triple Anvil Press at Mystery Ridge
P. O. Box 7050
Ann Arbor, MI 48107

To the Reader

This brief introduction to *A Reproduction in Facsimile of Hamlet from the First Folio of 1623* has three purposes. The first is to place the 1623 First Folio in the context of the years of publishing of Shakespeare's plays prior to 1623, which saw only half of the plays become available in print. The second is to provide a perspective of the three texts of *Hamlet*, the short 1st Quarto (the so-called *bad quarto*), and the two more accepted texts, the 2nd Quarto of 1604/5 and the First Folio. The final purpose is to alert Shakespeare enthusiasts to the remarkable differences between the texts of the 2nd Quarto and the Folio.

Most of the popular editions of *Hamlet* are conflations of the texts of the 2nd Quarto and the Folio, with occasional echoes of the 1st Quarto. This introduction provides an outline of some of the significant differences between the 2nd Quarto and the Folio, which should enhance the reader's appreciation of the facsimile.

Press sheets used in the First Folio were approximately 13 x 18 inches, prior to folding and trimming. The resulting pages of the extant copies are approximately the size of this facsimile. Some copies are smaller because of trimming in re-binding.

Shakespeare's Plays – Printers & Publishers of the Early Quartos

Revision L5b 2 October 2008

Related Plays

Title	Year	Printer	Publisher
The First Part of the Contention	1594	Creed	Millington
True Trag. Richard Duke of York	1595	Short	Millington
The True Trag. Of Richard Third	1594	Creed	Barley
The Taming of a Shrew	1594	Short	Burby (2nd edition in 1596)
Troublesome Raigne K.John Part 1,2	1591		Clarke (Part 2 reprinted in 1595)
The Famous Victories of Henry V	1598	Creed	

Shakespeare's Plays

Play	Approx Year	1st Quarto			2nd Quarto			3rd Quarto			Subsequent Quarto Printings through 1622
		Year	Printer	Publisher	Year	Printer	Publisher	Year	Printer	Publisher	
Henry VI, Part II	1590	1594 Published as indicated			1600	White	Millington				The Whole Contention Part 1 & 2 — 1619 Jaggard / Pavier "by william shake-speare gent." ↑ Q6 1622 Purfoot / Law
Henry VI, Part III	1590	1595 Published as indicated			1600	White	Millington				
Henry VI, Part I	1591										
Richard III	1592	1597	Simmes	Wise	1598	Creed	Wise	1602	Creed	Wise	1605 Creed Law; 1612 Creed Law
The Comedy of Errors	1592										
Titus Andronicus	1593	1594	Danter	White/Millgth	1600	Roberts	White	1611	Alde	White	
The Taming of the Shrew	1593							1607	Simmes	Ling	
Two Gentlemen Verona	1594										
Love's Labour's Lost	1594	1598	White	Burby							
Romeo and Juliet	1594	1597*	Danter		1599	Creed	Burby	1609	Windt	Smethwick	
Richard II	1595	1597	Simmes	Wise	1598	Simmes	Wise (2 issues)	1608	White	Law (2 issues)	2nd Issue Undated (1822-1624); 1615 Purfoot Law; 1619 White Law (falsely dated 1600**); 1622 Jaggard Mathewes / Pavier Dewe
Midsummer Night's Drm	1595	1600	Bradock	Fisher							
King John	1596							1611	Simmes	Helme (by w.sh. / by w.shakespeare)	1608 Windt Law; 1613 White Law (Troublesome Raigne of King John: 1622 Mathewes)
The Merchant of Venice	1596	1600	Roberts	Hayes							
Henry IV, Part I	1597	1598^F	Short	Wise	1599	Stafford	Wise	1604	Simmes	Law	1613 White Law; Q6 1622 Purfoot / Law
Henry IV, Part II	1597	1600	Simmes	Wise/Aspley							
Henry V	1598	1600*	Creed	Mil/Busby; 1600 Simmes Wise/Aspley	1602	Creed	Pavier	1619 (falsely dated 1608**)			The Famous Victories of Henry V — 1617 Alsop Barlow (2 issues)
Much Ado About Nothing	1598										
Julius Caesar	1599										
As You Like It	1599										
Twelfth Night	1599										
Hamlet	1600	1603*	Simmes	Ling/Trndl	1604/5^V	Roberts	Ling	1611	Eld	Smethwick	Undated 1622?; 1619 Jaggard Smethwick / Johnson
Merry Wives of Windsor	1600	1602*	Creed	Johnson	1619	Jaggard					
Troilus and Cressida	1601	1609	Eld	Bonian/Walley							
All's Well T Ends Well	1602										
Measure for Measure	1604										
Othello	1604	1622	Oakes	Walkley							
King Lear	1605	1608^V	Oakes	Butter (known as the Pied Bull Quarto)	1619	Jaggard	Pavier (falsely dated 1608**)				1619 Jaggard Pavier (falsely dated 1608**); N. Butter falsely designated as publisher but without Pied Bull location
Macbeth	1605										
Antony & Cleopatra	1606										
Coriolanus	1607										
Timon of Athens	1607										
Pericles (not in 1st Folio-F)	1608	1609*	White/Creed	Gosson	1609*	White/Creed	Gosson	1611		Stafford	1619 Jaggard Pavier
Cymbeline	1609										
The Winter's Tale	1610										
The Tempest	1611										
Henry VIII	1612										
Two Noble Kinsmen (not in F)	1612										

The Chronicle History of King Leir	1605	Stafford	Wright

Partial List of Printers
Edward Alde — Peter Short
Bernard Alsop — Valentine Simmes
Richard Bradock — Simon Stafford
Thomas Creed — William White
John Danter — John Windt
George Eld
W & I. Jaggard
Aug. Mathewes
Nicholas Oakes
Thomas Purfoot
James Roberts

Partial List of Publishers
William Aspley — Thomas Fisher
William Barley — Henry Gossen
Timothy Barlow — John Helme
Richard Bonian — Thomas Hayes
Cuthbert Burby — W & I Jaggard
John Busby — Arthur Johnson
Nathaniel Butter — Edward White
Sampson Clarke — Matthew Law — Andrew Wise
Thomas Dewe — Nicholas Ling — John Wright
Thomas Millington

* So-called Bad Quartos
^F Fragment (Q0) predates Q1
^V Significant Variant vs. Folio

** Some of the 1619 Jaggard / Pavier Quartos carry earlier dates, and some of these carry the names of their earlier printers and publishers

Printer sequences: Wise to Law Roberts to Jaggard White to Matthews
Publisher sequences: Ling to Smethwicke Creed to Alsop

Title Page images from 19th century Griggs and Praetorius facsimiles
© Charles Adams Kelly and Howland Research, LLC - howlandresearch.com

Figure 1

Variant Texts and the Texts of *Hamlet*

The graphic in Figure 1 lists Shakespeare's plays. Thirty six of the 38 plays listed appeared in the First Folio. The two missing plays, *Pericles* and *The Two Noble Kinsmen* were either thought to be collaborative works, or copyrights could not be obtained. As the graphic illustrates, half of Shakespeare's plays were printed individually, in the smaller quarto format, prior to 1623.

Since many of Shakespeare's plays were preserved only by publication in the First Folio, the Folio is considered the most important book in English literature. And, since the Folio was edited by Shakespeare's fellow players, John Heminges and Henry Condell, the Folio texts carry considerable authority.

Shakespeare died in 1616, seven years before publication of the Folio. As indicated, nineteen of the 38 plays had appeared separately in the smaller quarto format, prior to 1623. Since the texts of several of these quartos were variant, the editors lamented *that the author had not lived to have set forth and overseen his own writings.* This helps account for the uncertainty that surrounds the variant texts of several plays.

To the left, in Figure 1, seven *related plays* are identified. These plays, of unknown authorship, were printed and published by several of the people associated with the printing and publishing of Shakespeare's plays. The *related plays* may have been owned by Shakespeare's company, and Shakespeare may have contributed to the creation or refinement of some of them.

Turning to *Hamlet*, most Shakespeare enthusiasts are aware of the short text of 1603, the so-called *bad quarto* of 1603. But, many are intrigued to learn that there are *two* texts of *Hamlet*, accepted as *good*, the 2nd Quarto of 1604/5 and the Folio.

In Figure 1, only the first and second quartos of *Hamlet* are highlighted, indicating that they represent two different texts. *Hamlet* appeared two additional times prior to 1623, but the quarto of 1611 and the undated quarto, thought to have been printed in 1622, were both based on the 2nd Quarto.

The short text of the 1st Quarto of 1603 is often referred to as a *bad quarto*. Many believe it is an *unauthorized* abridgement of Shakespeare's text, created in part by the actor who played the part of Marcellus. The Marcellus lines are very similar in both the 1st and 2nd Quartos. Of course, if Shakespeare simply elected not to change this part when revising and expanding an earlier version of *Hamlet*, this would account for the similarity in the lines, also. The possibility that the 1st Quarto is a predecessor text, with some degree of Shakespearian collaboration, is a theory under a new cycle of investigation.

The Three Texts of

SHAKESPEARE'S HAMLET

Q1 1603   Q2 1604/5   FOLIO 1623

Figure 2
Text Graphic illustrating 45% less text in Q1, larger passages unique to Q2 or F, and displacement of major scene in Q1.

The First Folio of *Hamlet* in Perspective

In Figure 2, the shaded areas in each column represent lines of text in the three *significant* texts of *Hamlet*: the 1st Quarto of 1603, the 2nd Quarto of 1604/5, and the Folio of 1623. For convenience, scholars designate the quartos as Q1 and Q2. The date of Q2 is designated as 1604/5 because three of the extant copies have title pages dated 1604 while four are dated 1605, though all seven are from a single printing by James Roberts. Many textual scholars designate the Folio as F or *the Folio*, rather than F1, for the reason that no folio edition beyond the First Folio has any independent textual authority.

As indicated by the gaps in the first column in the Figure, one can estimate that the text of Q1 is about 45% short by comparison. The Figure also indicates the shift in location of the *To be* soliloquy and the *Nunnery scene* in the 1st Quarto. The texts of both Q2 and the Folio are similar in length, but there are significant *missing* increments that appear as gaps in one column or the other. And, there are over 900 lesser variants which do not show on such a compressed scale.

In transcribing the drafts of Shakespeare's plays, at least one professional scribe was known to have made refinements to the texts. The *fair copy*, authorial or scribal, went to both the censor and the theater company. Changes made during the assigning of roles could have been a mix of authorial refinements and acting company alterations. And, when a text passed to the printing house and its compositors and proof readers, the text was quite beyond the control of the author.

Considering the inconsistencies in the play quartos, it has been supposed that Shakespeare had little care about the printing of his plays, nor control over them when they passed to the printer. The financial model of quarto printing may account for this. Authorial review of the compositors' work would have added expense. Plays could go out of fashion quickly, so quartos were like pamphlets that had to be printed inexpensively. Publishers would not be likely to invest in the extra resources to produce high quality play quartos, as they would for a Bible printed in folio. Greater care and the comparative luxury of the folio format were reserved for more classic and timeless publications.

As this introduction narrows its focus to the remarkable differences between Q2 and the Folio, readers should be aware that there has always been an undercurrent of respect for Q1 and the possibility that it represents a predecessor text, rather than a pirated abridgement. The fact that Nicholas Ling published both the *bad* Q1 and the good Q2, is one of those items of evidence that prevents scholars from dismissing Q1 out of hand. The echoes of Q1, particularly in the area of stage direction, add to the possibility that Shakespeare had a hand in all three texts. In the case of Q2 and the Folio, several of the variants appear to reflect more than the whims of actors, compositors, or others.

Lines of Dialogue Unique to Q2 vs. F and F vs. Q2

3x2 Page	Act.Scn.Ln	TLN	Q2	F	Description of Passage
4	1.1.108	125	18		Hora. Julius fell...sheeted dead
7	1.2.58	238	⠛		Polo. I sealed my hard consent.
14	1.3.18	479		1	Laer. For he himself is subject to his birth.
17 & 18	1.4.17	623	22		Ham. Carrying, I say the stamp of one defect
19	1.4.75	664	4		Hora. That looks so many fathoms to the sea
26	2.1.53	946		1	Reynol. At friend, or so, or Gentlemen.
29	2.2.17	1036	1		King...to us unknowne afflicts him thus
37	2.2.220	1255		1	Pol. And sodainely contrive the meanes of meeting
37 & 38	2.2.275	1285		32	Ham. Denmark's a prison
40	2.2.338	1384		22	Rosen. ...an ayrie of Children, little Yases
53	3.2.116	1968		2	Ham. I meane, my Head upon your Lap?
55	3.2.167	2036	3		Player Queen. For women feare too much, (extra line)
55	3.2.171	2041	2		Player Queen. Where love is great
56	3.2.218	2086	2		Player Queen. To desperation turne...
57	3.2.272	2135		1	Ham. What, frighted with false fire.
63	3.4.5	2381		1	Ham. Mother, mother, mother.
65	3.4.72	2456	8		Ham. Eyes without feeling, feeling without sight
67	3.4.161	2543	7		Ham. That monster custome
68	3.4.179	2555	1		Ham. Onr word more good Lady.
68	3.4.203	2577	9		Ham. Ther's letters seald
69	4.1.4	2590	1		Ger. Bestow this place on us a little while.
70	4.1.41	2628	2		King. Whose whisper ore the worlds dyameter
71	4.2.26	2689	⠛		Ham. A man may fish with the worme that hath eate of
73 & 74	4.4.9	2743	59		Cap. A little patch of ground
79	4.5.165	2914		3	Laer. Nature is fine in Love
82	4.7.37	3046		1	King. How now? What Newes?
82	4.7.40	3050	1		Messen, Of him that brought them.
83	4.7.69	3079	15		Laertes. My Lord I will be rul'd,
84	4.7.101	3099	2		King. He swore had neither...
84	4.7.114	3115	10		King. There lives within the very flame of love
87	5.1.41	3223		3	Clo. Could hee digge without Armes?
88	5.1.114	3297		1	Ham. Is this the find of his Fines...
95	5.2.69	3572		15	Ham. And is't not to be damn'd
95 & 96	5.2.106	3594	30		Cour. ...an absolute gentlemen
97 & 98	5.2.195	3655	12		Lord. The Queen desires you...entertainment
98	5.2.242	3692		1	Ham. Sir, in this Audience,
			215	85	Total Lines of Dialogue in Q2 and F Unique Passages

3x2 Pages: *The Hamlet 3x2 Text Research Toolset*, Triple Anvil Press, 2008

Act.Scn.Ln: *The Riverside Shakespeare*

TLN's: *The Norton Facsimile The First Folio of Shakespeare*, © W. W. Norton & Company, 1968

Line Counts: **Bold** indicates larger passages   Shaded Cells indicate passages believed to be in Folio manuscript

Figure 3

The Uniqueness of Folio *Hamlet*

Figure 3 shows the locations of full lines and passages unique to either Q2 or the Folio text. There are over 200 lines that are unique to Q2, and over 90 that are unique to the Folio. Most of these lines appear in 10 large passages unique to Q2 and three large passages that are unique to the Folio text. The first foldout shows the location of these 13 passages in the context of the plot elements of *Hamlet*. The second foldout provides the text of each. Not shown on the foldouts are the 21 passages of only 1-3 lines each and the hundreds of variants involving single words.

Many enthusiasts are startled to learn that the text of *Hamlet*, in their favorite edition, is neither the text of Q2 nor the Folio, but rather a conflated text, and that Hamlet's final soliloquy, *How all occasions do inform against me,* is absent from the Folio text, the text they had assumed to be the ultimate authority. An editor's assumption might be that the omission was the result of a compositor's oversight. But, if changes are part of a pattern, one might conclude that Shakespeare himself made the changes as he refined Q2 to produce the text of Folio *Hamlet*.

Some of the additions and deletions appear to be related. In the Folio text, Hamlet says, *I am very sorry...that to Leartes I forgot my selfe...Ile count* (court) *his favors.* Since Hamlet's desire to make peace with Laertes now springs from within himself, the Queen's instruction of him to do so could have been eliminated as the Folio text was created, as could Hamlet's Q2 derision of Laertes. Additionally, the character of Laertes is softened by the elimination of his request to be the *organ* of Hamlet's demise. Hamlet's Q2 distrust of Rosencrantz and Guildenstern has been eliminated in the Folio, also. Perhaps the intention was to move the focus outside of Hamlet's brooding to improve the suspense.

Also, late in the Folio text, Hamlet proclaims, *And is't not to be damn'd to let this canker of our nature come to further evill.* By concluding that there is divine justice in revenging his father's murder, Hamlet seems to have solved the complex problem of secular honor and divine justice. Upon adding these few lines, Shakespeare may have concluded that Hamlet's Q2 lines on the *vicious mole of nature* (tragic flaw) could be eliminated. Shakespeare may have concluded that the theory of a tragic flaw was too narrow a theory to contain the character of Claudius.

Additionally, Shakespeare may have come to believe that Hamlet's Q2 soliloquy, *How all occasions doe informe against me,* missing from the Folio text, was bringing too much of the focus on Hamlet's state of mind, as opposed to the action of the plot. This and other alterations to the text of Q2, whether by Shakespeare or other hands, may have been intended to improve the flow of action in *The Tragedie of Hamlet, Prince of Denmarke* as represented by the Folio text.

A *Folio in Sixes*

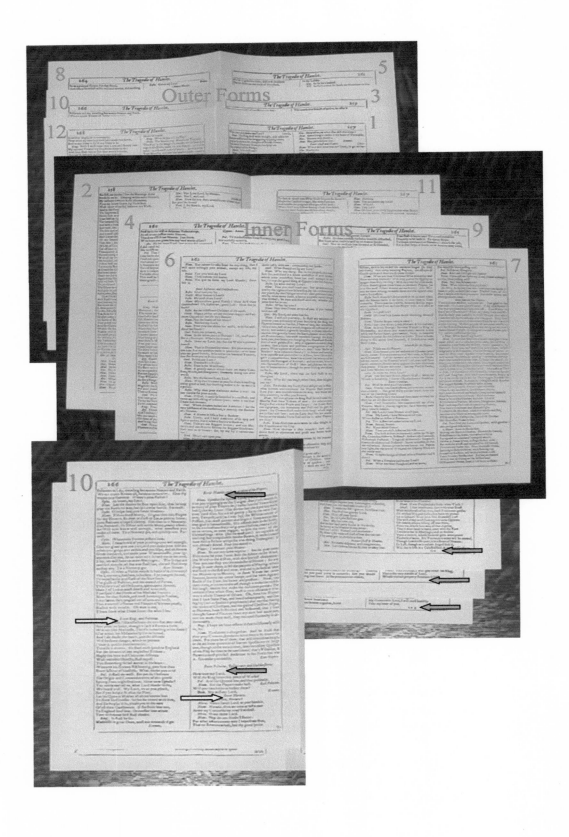

Figure 4
A Folio in Sixes

4.

A *Folio in Sixes*

The Folio is predominately a *folio in sixes*, meaning that it was made up of sets of three press sheets, folded and nested making *quires*, of six leaves or 12 pages. The pages were printed by formes, meaning that type was set for each pair of pages on each side of each press sheet. As Figure 4 indicates, the two pages printed simultaneously on the inside or outside of each press sheet, are referred to as the *inner* or *outer forme*.

The only consecutive pages that would be printed next to each other on a press sheet would be the sixth and seventh, the *inner forme* pages of the inner-most press sheet. The *outer forme* of the outer-most press sheet would carry pages 1 and 12. The assembled quire was sometimes called a *gathering*. During actual production, while one press sheet was being printed, the type for the next forme was being set. With a limited quantity of type, the type for the first printed pair of pages was *distributed* back into the type *cases*, long before type was set for the final pair of pages in the quire. This necessitated a process of estimating how much manuscript copy would fill each quire, and each page, a process called *casting off*.

Manuscript copy was marked by anticipated page break points. The compositors, often working in pairs, began by setting type for the sixth and seventh pages. As progress was made toward the forme for the first and twelfth pages, the compositors might be forced to stretch the layout to fill potential gaps, or compress lines to save space. The fifth through the first pages were the most critical because they were set in reverse order. Therefore, any type spacing problem with one of these pages could not be resolved by forcing it forward to the nest page, because the following page had already been set and perhaps printed.

In the text of Folio *Hamlet*, there are no extreme cases of this, but the reader will notice that on page 266 the copy did not fill the page. The compositor inserted *white lines* or blank spaces following two of the four lines of stage direction. Most readers overlook the inconsistency in layout, which is indicated by red vs. yellow arrows in the Figure. Many pages have some trace of compositor adjustment.

Note that the page numbers jump from 156 to 257, perhaps the miss-interpretation of page numbers noted during the casting off process. Page 257 is the first page of a new quire. This miss-numbering of pages would not have caused inconvenience in gathering. Press sheets were gathered by a press sheet code on the front page of each *outer forme*. For the three press sheets on the oo quire, one would expect to find the designations oo, oo2, and oo3, on pages 257, 259, and 261. As indicated by the set of three arrows, oo2 is missing from page 259. This may have caused inconvenience when the press sheets were gathered. The text of *Hamlet*, in the Folio, occupies two complete quires, preceded and followed by portions of two others.

Afterword

Hamlet's soliloquy, *How all occasions doe informe against me,* does not appear in the Folio text. If Q2 had not been printed, this famous soliloquy would have been lost to the history of literature. Near the end of this soliloquy there are lines speaking of *the imminent death of twenty thousand men...goe to their graves...fight for a plot whereon the numbers cannot try the cause.* If this was a bitter reflection on the ill-fated Essex campaign in Ireland, the thought may have been current in 1604, the time of Q2, but it is absent from the text of the 1623 Folio.

The absence of this significant soliloquy from the Folio text and the addition of another soliloquy could have been motivated by the fading memory of the Essex campaign, the issue of honor vs. salvation, or to improve the flow of the action. The change could have been made by Shakespeare, by the actors, or requested by the censor. Consider that perhaps both the *how all occasions* (Q2) and the *is't not to be damn'd* (Folio) soliloquies were present in the manuscript, and that the Folio compositors simply miss-read a notation and failed to allow space for the Q2 soliloquy when counting their lines. This is but one of the unanswerable questions concerning Shakespeare's intentions.

Among the selected preliminary pages of the Folio, is the message *To the great Variety of Readers* from the editors John Heminges and Henry Condell. Much is made of the statement *His mind and hand went together...we have scarce received...a blot in his papers.* This has been seized upon by some as evidence that Shakespeare created only one master text of each of his plays, and that variants are the products of scribes, censors, actors, compositors, proof readers, and others through whose hands the texts passed. There is much evidence to the contrary, including the wish expressed by the editors in the same statement, *that the author himself had lived to have set forth, and overseen his own writings.* Scholarship is more accepting of the idea that Shakespeare may have revised his plays.

Also included among the preliminary pages is the *Catalogue* or index. Readers may notice that the *Catalogue* lists only 35 of the 36 plays included in the Folio. The Folio publishers believed they would be unable to obtain the rights to *Troilus and Cressida* at the time they printed the *Catalogue*.

Enjoy the facsimile of Folio *Hamlet* that you hold in your hands. The publishers have made every effort to create an artifact worthy of your attention and use as an enthusiast or as a scholar. Part of the intrigue of comparing this facsimile with any popular edition, is the speculation over the source of the textual variants.

Ann Arbor   C.A.K.
March 2009

Mr. WILLIAM
SHAKESPEARES

COMEDIES,
HISTORIES, &
TRAGEDIES.

Published according to the True Originall Copies.

Martin Droeshout sculpsit London.

LONDON
Printed by Isaac Iaggard, and Ed. Blount. 1623.

To the great Variety of Readers.

Rom the moſt able, to him that can but ſpell: There you are number'd. We had rather you were weighd. Eſpecially, when the fate of all Bookes depends vpon your capacities : and not of your heads alone, but of your purſes. Well ! It is now publique, & you wil ſtand for your priuiledges wee know : to read, and cenſure. Do ſo, but buy it firſt. That doth beſt commend a Booke, the Stationer ſaies. Then, how odde ſoeuer your braines be, or your wiſedomes, make your licence the ſame, and ſpare not. Iudge your ſixe-pen'orth, your ſhillings worth, your fiue ſhillings worth at a time, or higher, ſo you riſe to the iuſt rates, and welcome. But, what euer you do, Buy. Cenſure will not driue a Trade, or make the Iacke go. And though you be a Magiſtrate of wit, and ſit on the Stage at *Black-Friers*, or the *Cock-pit*, to arraigne Playes dailie, know, theſe Playes haue had their triall alreadie, and ſtood out all Appeales ; and do now come forth quitted rather by a Decree of Court, then any purchas'd Letters of commendation.

It had bene a thing, we confeſſe, worthie to haue bene wiſhed, that the Author himſelfe had liu'd to haue ſet forth, and ouerſeen his owne writings ; But ſince it hath bin ordain'd otherwiſe, and he by death departed from that right, we pray you do not envie his Friends, the office of their care, and paine, to haue collected & publiſh'd them ; and ſo to haue publiſh'd them, as where (before) you were abus'd with diuerſe ſtolne, and ſurreptitious copies, maimed, and deformed by the frauds and ſtealthes of iniurious impoſtors, that expos'd them : euen thoſe, are now offer'd to your view cur'd, and perfect of their limbes ; and all the reſt, abſolute in their numbers, as he conceiued thē. Who, as he was a happie imitator of Nature, was a moſt gentle expreſſer of it. His mind and hand went together : And what he thought, he vttered with that eaſineſſe, that wee haue ſcarſe receiued from him a blot in his papers. But it is not our prouince, who onely gather his works, and giue them you, to praiſe him. It is yours that reade him. And there we hope, to your diuers capacities, you will finde enough, both to draw, and hold you : for his wit can no more lie hid, then it could be loſt. Reade him, therefore ; and againe, and againe : And if then you doe not like him, ſurely you are in ſome manifeſt danger, not to vnderſtand him. And ſo we leaue you to other of his Friends, whom if you need, can bee your guides : if you neede them not, you can leade your ſelues, and others. And ſuch Readers we wiſh him.

Iohn Heminge.
Henrie Condell.

A CATALOGVE

of the seuerall Comedies, Histories, and Tragedies contained in this Volume.

The Workes of William Shakefpeare,

containing all his Comedies, Hiftories, and Tragedies : Truely fet forth, according to their firft *ORJGJNALL*.

The Names of the Principall Actors
in all thefe Playes.

Illiam Shakefpeare.

Richard Burbadge.

John Hemmings.

Auguftine Phillips.

William Kempt.

Thomas Poope.

George Bryan.

Henry Condell.

William Slye.

Richard Cowly.

John Lowine.

Samuell Croffe.

Alexander Cooke.

Samuel Gilburne.

Robert Armin.

William Oftler.

Nathan Field.

John Underwood.

Nicholas Tooley.

William Eccleftone.

Jofeph Taylor.

Robert Benfield.

Robert Goughe.

Richard Robinfon.

Iohn Shancke.

Iohn Rice.

Folio *Hamlet*

In the actual pages of the Folio of 1623,
The Tragedie of Hamlet, Prince of Denmarke
begins on the verso of the last page of *Macbeth*.

To accurately reflect this arrangement,
these facsimile pages of *Hamlet*
begin on the following page.

THE TRAGEDIE OF
HAMLET, Prince of Denmarke.

Actus Primus. Scœna Prima.

Enter Barnardo and Francisco two Centinels.

Barnardo.

WHo's there?

Fran. Nay answer me: Stand & vnfold
your selfe.

Bar. Long liue the King.

Fran. Barnardo?

Bar. He.

Fran. You come most carefully vpon your houre.

Bar. 'Tis now strook twelue, get thee to bed Francisco.

Fran. For this releefe much thankes: 'Tis bitter cold,
And I am sicke at heart.

Barn. Haue you had quiet Guard?

Fran. Not a Mouse stirring.

Barn. Well, goodnight. If you do meet Horatio and
Marcellus, the Riuals of my Watch, bid them make hast.

Enter Horatio and Marcellus.

Fran. I thinke I heare them. Stand: who's there?

Hor. Friends to this ground.

Mar. And Leige-men to the Dane.

Fran. Giue you good night.

Mar. O farwel honest Soldier, who hath relieu'd you?

Fra. Barnardo ha's my place: giue you goodnight.

Exit Fran.

Mar. Holla Barnardo.

Bar. Say, what is Horatio there?

Hor. A peece of him.

Bar. Welcome Horatio, welcome good Marcellus.

Mar. What, ha's this thing appear'd againe to night.

Bar. I haue seene nothing.

Mar. Horatio saies, 'tis but our Fantasie,
And will not let beleefe take hold of him
Touching this dreaded sight, twice seene of vs,
Therefore I haue intreated him along
With vs, to watch the minutes of this Night,
That if againe this Apparition come,
He may approue our eyes, and speake to it.

Hor. Tush, tush, 'twill not appeare.

Bar. Sit downe a-while,
And let vs once againe assaile your eares,
That are so fortified against our Story,
What we two Nights haue seene.

Hor. Well, sit we downe,
And let vs heare Barnardo speake of this.

Barn. Last night of all,
When yond same Starre that's Westward from the Pole
Had made his course t'illume that part of Heauen

Where now it burnes, Marcellus and my selfe,
The Bell then beating one.

Mar. Peace, breake thee of: *Enter the Ghost.*
Looke where it comes againe.

Barn. In the same figure, like the King that's dead.

Mar. Thou art a Scholler; speake to it Horatio.

Barn. Lookes it not like the King? Marke it Horatio.

Hora. Most like: It harrowes me with fear & wonder

Barn. It would be spoke too.

Mar. Question it Horatio.

Hor. What art thou that vsurp'st this time of night,
Together with that Faire and Warlike forme
In which the Maiesty of buried Denmarke
Did sometimes march: By Heauen I charge thee speake.

Mar. It is offended.

Barn. See, it stalkes away.

Hor. Stay: speake; speake: I Charge thee, speake.

Exit the Ghost.

Mar. 'Tis gone, and will not answer.

Barn. How now Horatio? You tremble & look pale:
Is not this something more then Fantasie?
What thinke you on't?

Hor. Before my God, I might not this beleeue
Without the sensible and true auouch
Of mine owne eyes.

Mar. Is it not like the King?

Hor. As thou art to thy selfe,
Such was the very Armour he had on,
When th'Ambitious Norwey combatted:
So frown'd he once, when in an angry parle
He smot the sledded Pollax on the Ice.
'Tis strange.

Mar. Thus twice before, and iust at this dead houre,
With Martiall stalke, hath he gone by our Watch.

Hor. In what particular thought to work, I know not:
But in the grosse and scope of my Opinion,
This boades some strange erruption to our State.

Mar. Good now sit downe, & tell me he that knowes
Why this same strict and most obseruant Watch,
So nightly toyles the subiect of the Land,
And why such dayly Cast of Brazon Cannon
And Forraigne Mart for Implements of warre:
Why such impresse of Ship-wrights, whose sore Taske
Do's not diuide the Sunday from the weeke,
What might be toward, that this sweaty hast
Doth make the Night ioynt-Labourer with the day:
Who is't that can informe me?

Hor. That can I,

At

At least the whisper goes so : Our last King,
Whose Image euen but now appear'd to vs,
Was (as you know) by *Fortinbras* of Norway,
(Thereto prick'd on by a most emulate Pride)
Dar'd to the Combate. In which, our Valiant *Hamlet*,
(For so this side of our knowne world esteem'd him)
Did slay this *Fortinbras* : who by a Seal'd Compact,
Well ratified by Law, and Heraldrie,
Did forfeite (with his life) all those his Lands
Which he stood seiz'd on, to the Conqueror :
Against the which, a Moity competent
Was gaged by our King : which had return'd
To the Inheritance of *Fortinbras*,
Had he bin Vanquisher, as by the same Cou'nant
And carriage of the Article designe,
His fell to *Hamlet*. Now sir, young *Fortinbras*,
Of vnimproued Mettle, hot and full,
Hath in the skirts of Norway, heere and there,
Shark'd vp a List of Landlesse Resolutes,
For Foode and Diet, to some Enterprize
That hath a stomacke in't : which is no other
(And it doth well appeare vnto our State)
But to recouer of vs by strong hand
And termes Compulsatiue, those foresaid Lands
So by his Father lost : and this (I take it)
Is the maine Motiue of our Preparations,
The Sourse of this our Watch, and the cheefe head
Of this post-hast, and Romage in the Land.

Enter Ghost againe.

But soft, behold : Loe, where it comes againe :
Ile crosse it, though it blast me. Stay Illusion :
If thou hast any sound, or vse of Voyce,
Speake to me. If there be any good thing to be done,
That may to thee do ease, and grace to me ; speak to me.
If thou art priuy to thy Countries Fate
(Which happily foreknowing may auoyd) Oh speake.
Or, if thou hast vp-hoorded in thy life
Extorted Treasure in the wombe of Earth,
(For which, they say, you Spirits oft walke in death)
Speake of it. Stay, and speake. Stop it *Marcellus*.

Mar. Shall I strike at it with my Partizan ?
Hor. Do, if it will not stand.
Barn. 'Tis heere.
Hor. 'Tis heere.
Mar. 'Tis gone.   *Exit Ghost.*

We do it wrong, being so Maiesticall
To offer it the shew of Violence,
For it is as the Ayre, invulnerable,
And our vaine blowes, malicious Mockery.

Barn. It was about to speake, when the Cocke crew.
Hor. And then it started, like a guilty thing
Vpon a fearfull Summons. I haue heard,
The Cocke that is the Trumpet to the day,
Doth with his lofty and shrill-sounding Throate
Awake the God of Day : and at his warning,
Whether in Sea, or Fire, in Earth, or Ayre,
Th'extrauagant, and erring Spirit, hyes
To his Confine. And of the truth heerein,
This present Obiect made probation.

Mar. It faded on the crowing of the Cocke.
Some sayes, that euer 'gainst that Season comes
Wherein our Sauiours Birth is celebrated,
The Bird of Dawning singeth all night long :
And then (they say) no Spirit can walke abroad,
The nights are wholsome, then no Planets strike,
No Faiery talkes, nor Witch hath power to Charme :

So hallow'd, and so gracious is the time.
Hor. So haue I heard, and do in part beleeue it.
But looke, the Morne in Russet mantle clad,
Walkes o're the dew of yon high Easterne Hill,
Breake we our Watch vp, and by my aduice
Let vs impart what we haue seene to night
Vnto yong *Hamlet*. For vpon my life,
This Spirit dumbe to vs, will speake to him :
Do you consent we shall acquaint him with it,
As needfull in our Loues, fitting our Duty ?
Mar. Let do't I pray, and I this morning know
Where we shall finde him most conueniently. *Exeunt*

Scena Secunda.

*Enter Claudius King of Denmarke, Gertrude the Queene,
Hamlet, Polonius, Laertes, and his Sister O-
phelia, Lords Attendant.*

King. Though yet of *Hamlet* our deere Brothers death
The memory be greene : and that it vs befitted
To beare our hearts in greefe, and our whole Kingdome
To be contracted in one brow of woe :
Yet so farre hath Discretion fought with Nature,
That we with wisest sorrow thinke on him,
Together with remembrance of our selues.
Therefore our sometimes Sister, now our Queen,
Th'Imperiall Ioyntresse of this warlike State,
Haue we, as 'twere, with a defeated ioy,
With one Auspicious, and one Dropping eye,
With mirth in Funerall, and with Dirge in Marriage,
In equall Scale weighing Delight and Dole
Taken to Wife ; nor haue we heerein barr'd
Your better Wisedomes, which haue freely gone
With this affaire along, for all our Thankes.
Now followes, that you know young *Fortinbras*,
Holding a weake supposall of our worth ;
Or thinking by our late deere Brothers death,
Our State to be disioynt, and out of Frame,
Colleagued with the dreame of his Aduantage ;
He hath not fayl'd to pester vs with Message,
Importing the surrender of those Lands
Lost by his Father : with all Bonds of Law
To our most valiant Brother. So much for him.

Enter Voltemand and Cornelius.

Now for our selfe, and for this time of meeting
Thus much the businesse is. We haue heere writ
To Norway, Vncle of young *Fortinbras*,
Who Impotent and Bedrid, scarsely heares
Of this his Nephewes purpose, to suppresse
His further gate heerein. In that the Leuies,
The Lists, and full proportions are all made
Out of his subiect : and we heere dispatch
You good *Cornelius*, and you *Voltemand*,
For bearing of this greeting to old Norway,
Giuing to you no further personall power
To businesse with the King, more then the scope
Of these dilated Articles allow :
Farewell, and let your hast commend your duty.
Volt. In that, and all things, will we shew our duty.
King. We doubt it nothing, heartily farewell.

Exit Voltemand and Cornelius.

And now *Laertes*, what's the newes with you ?

You

You told vs of some suite. What is't *Laertes* ?
You cannot speake of Reason to the Dane,
And loose your voyce. What would'st thou beg *Laertes*,
That shall not be my Offer, not thy Asking ?
The Head is not more Natiue to the Heart,
The Hand more Instrumentall to the Mouth,
Then is the Throne of Denmarke to thy Father.
What would'st thou haue *Laertes* ?

    Laer. Dread my Lord,
Your leaue and fauour to returne to France,
From whence, though willingly I came to Denmarke
To shew my duty in your Coronation,
Yet now I must confesse, that duty done,
My thoughts and wishes bend againe towards France,
And bow them to your gracious leaue and pardon.

    King. Haue you your Fathers leaue ?
What sayes *Pollonius* ?

    Pol. He hath my Lord:
I do beseech you giue him leaue to go.

    King. Take thy faire houre *Laertes*, time be thine,
And thy best graces spend it at thy will :
But now my Cosin *Hamlet*, and my Sonne ?

    Ham. A little more then kin, and lesse then kinde.

    King. How is it that the Clouds still hang on you ?

    Ham. Not so my Lord, I am too much i'th'Sun.

    Queen. Good *Hamlet* cast thy nightly colour off,
And let thine eye looke like a Friend on Denmarke.
Do not for euer with thy veyled lids
Seeke for thy Noble Father in the dust ;
Thou know'st 'tis common, all that liues must dye,
Passing through Nature, to Eternity.

    Ham. I Madam, it is common.

    Queen. If it be ;
Why seemes it so particular with thee.

    Ham. Seemes Madam? Nay, it is : I know not Seemes :
'Tis not alone my Inky Cloake (good Mother)
Nor Customary suites of solemne Blacke,
Nor windy suspiration of forc'd breath,
No, nor the fruitfull Riuer in the Eye,
Nor the deiected hauiour of the Visage,
Together with all Formes, Moods, shewes of Griefe,
That can denote me truly. These indeed Seeme,,
For they are actions that a man might play :
But I haue that Within, which passeth show ;
These, but the Trappings, and the Suites of woe.

    King. 'Tis sweet and commendable
In your Nature *Hamlet*,
To giue these mourning duties to your Father :
But you must know, your Father lost a Father,
That Father lost, lost his, and the Suruiuer bound
In filiall Obligation, for some terme
To do obsequious Sorrow. But to perseuer
In obstinate Condolement, is a course
Of impious stubbornnesse. 'Tis vnmanly greefe,
It shewes a will most incorrect to Heauen,
A Heart vnfortified, a Minde impatient,
An Vnderstanding simple, and vnschool'd :
For, what we know must be, and is as common
As any the most vulgar thing to sence,
Why should we in our peeuish Opposition
Take it to heart ? Fye, 'tis a fault to Heauen,
A fault against the Dead, a fault to Nature,
To Reason most absurd, whose common Theame
Is death of Fathers, and who still hath cried,
From the first Coarse, till he that dyed to day,
This must be so. We pray you throw to earth

This vnpreuayling woe, and thinke of vs
As of a Father ; For let the world take note,
You are the most immediate to our Throne,
And with no lesse Nobility of Loue,
Then that which deerest Father beares his Sonne,
Do I impart towards you. For your intent
In going backe to Schoole in Wittenberg,
It is most retrograde to our desire :
And we beseech you, bend you to remaine
Heere in the cheere and comfort of our eye,
Our cheefest Courtier Cosin, and our Sonne.

    Qu. Let not thy Mother lose her Prayers *Hamlet* :
I prythee stay with vs, go not to Wittenberg.

    Ham. I shall in all my best
Obey you Madam.

    King. Why 'tis a louing, and a faire Reply,
Be as our selfe in Denmarke. Madam come,
This gentle and vnforc'd accord of *Hamlet*
Sits smiling to my heart ; in grace whereof,
No iocond health that Denmarke drinkes to day,
But the great Cannon to the Clowds shall tell,
And the Kings Rouce, the Heauens shall bruite againe,
Respeaking earthly Thunder. Come away.   *Exeunt*

Manet Hamlet.

    Ham. Oh that this too too solid Flesh, would melt,
Thaw, and resolue it selfe into a Dew :
Or that the Euerlasting had not fixt
His Cannon 'gainst Selfe-slaughter. O God, O God !
How weary, stale, flat, and vnprofitable
Seemes to me all the vses of this world ?
Fie on't ? Oh fie, fie, 'tis an vnweeded Garden
That growes to Seed : Things rank, and grosse in Nature
Posse sse it meerely. That it should come to this :
But two months dead : Nay, not so much ; not two,
So excellent a King, that was to this
Hyperion to a Satyre : so louing to my Mother,
That he might not beteene the windes of heauen
Visit her face too roughly. Heauen and Earth
Must I remember : why she would hang on him,
As if encrease of Appetite had growne
By what it fed on ; and yet within a month ?
Let me not thinke on't : Frailty, thy name is woman.
A little Month, or ere those shooes were old,
With which she followed my poore Fathers body
Like *Niobe*, all teares. Why she, euen she.
(O Heauen ! A beast that wants discourse of Reason
Would haue mourn'd longer) married with mine Vnkle,
My Fathers Brother : but no more like my Father,
Then I to *Hercules*. Within a Moneth ?
Ere yet the salt of most vnrighteous Teares
Had left the flushing of her gauled eyes,
She married. O most wicked speed, to post
With such dexterity to Incestuous sheets :
It is not, nor it cannot come to good.
But breake my heart, for I must hold my tongue.

Enter Horatio, Barnard, and Marcellus.

    Hor. Haile to your Lordship.

    Ham. I am glad to see you well :
Horatio, or I do forget my selfe.

    Hor. The same my Lord,
And your poore Seruant euer.

    Ham. Sir my good friend,
Ile change that name with you :
And what make you from Wittenberg *Horatio* ?

Marcellus.

Mar. My good Lord.

Ham. I am very glad to fee you: good euen Sir.
But what in faith make you from *Wittemberge* ?

Hor. A truant difpofition, good my Lord.

Ham. I would not haue your Enemy fay fo;
Nor fhall you doe mine eare that violence,
To make it trufter of your owne report
Againft your felfe. I know you are no Truant :
But what is your affaire in *Elfenour* ?
Wee'l teach you to drinke deepe,ere you depart.

Hor. My Lord,I came to fee your Fathers Funerall.

Ham. I pray thee doe not mock me (fellow Student)
I thinke it was to fee my Mothers Wedding.

Hor. Indeed my Lord,it followed hard vpon.

Ham. Thrift,thrift *Horatio:* the Funerall Bakt-meats
Did coldly furnifh forth the Marriage Tables ;
Would I had met my deareft foe in heauen,
Ere I had euer feene that day *Horatio.*
My father, me thinkes I fee my father.

Hor. Oh where my Lord?

Ham. In my minds eye (*Horatio*)

Hor. I faw him once; he was a goodly King.

Ham. He was a man, take him for all in all :
I fhall not look vpon his like againe.

Hor. My Lord, I thinke I faw him yefternight.

Ham. Saw? Who?

Hor. My Lord,the King your Father.

Ham. The King my Father?

Hor. Seafon your admiration for a while
With an attent eare; till I may deliuer
Vpon the witneffe of thefe Gentlemen,
This maruell to you.

Ham. For Heauens loue let me heare.

Hor. Two nights together,had thefe Gentlemen
(*Marcellus* and *Barnardo*) on their Watch
In the dead waft and middle of the night
Beene thus encountred. A figure like your Father,
Arm'd at all points exactly, *Cap a Pe*,
Appeares before them, and with follemne march
Goes flow and ftately : By them thrice he walkt,
By their oppreft and feare-furprized eyes,
Within his Truncheons length; whilft they beftil'd
Almoft to Ielly with the Act of feare,
Stand dumbe and fpeake not to him. This to me
In dreadfull fecrecie impart they did,
And I with them the third Night kept the Watch,
Whereas they had deliuer'd both in time,
Forme of the thing; each word made true and good,
The Apparition comes. I knew your Father :
Thefe hands are not more like.

Ham. But where was this ?

Mar. My Lord,vpon the platforme where we watcht.

Ham. Did you not fpeake to it?

Hor. My Lord, I did;
But anfwere made it none: yet once me thought
It lifted vp it head,and did addreffe
It felfe to motion, like as it would fpeake :
But euen then, the Morning Cocke crew lowd;
And at the found it fhrunke in haft away,
And vanifht from our fight.

Ham. Tis very ftrange.

Hor. As I doe liue my honourd Lord 'tis true;
And we did thinke it writ downe in our duty
To let you know of it.

Ham. Indeed, indeed Sirs; but this troubles me.

Hold you the watch to Night?

Both. We doe my Lord.

Ham. Arm'd, fay you?

Both. Arm'd, my Lord.

Ham. From top to toe?

Both. My Lord,from head to foote.

Ham. Then faw you not his face?

Hor. O yes, my Lord, he wore his Beauer vp.

Ham. What, lookt he frowningly?

Hor. A countenance more in forrow then in anger.

Ham. Pale,or red?

Hor. Nay very pale.

Ham. And fixt his eyes vpon you?

Hor. Moft conftantly.

Ham. I would I had beene there.

Hor. It would haue much amaz'd you.

Ham. Very like,very like : ftaid it long ?   (dred.

Hor. While one with moderate haft might tell a hun-

All. Longer,longer.

Hor. Not when I faw't.

Ham. His Beard was grifly? no.

Hor. It was, as I haue feene it in his life,
A Sable Siluer'd.
                                                    (gaine.

Ham. Ile watch to Night ; perchance 'twill wake a-

Hor. I warrant you it will.

Ham. If it affume my noble Fathers perfon,
Ile fpeake to it,though Hell it felfe fhould gape
And bid me hold my peace. I pray you all,
If you haue hitherto conceald this fight;
Let it bee treble in your filence ftill :
And whatfoeuer els fhall hap to night,
Giue it an vnderftanding but no tongue;
I will requite your loues ; fo, fare ye well :
Vpon the Platforme twixt eleuen and twelue,
Ile vifit you.

All. Our duty to your Honour.   *Exeunt.*

Ham. Your loue,as mine to you: farewell.
My Fathers Spirit in Armes ? All is not well:
I doubt fome foule play : would the Night were come;
Till then fit ftill my foule; foule deeds will rife,
Though all the earth orewhelm them to mens eies. *Exit.*

Scena Tertia.

Enter Laertes and Ophelia.

Laer. My neceffaries are imbark't; Farewell :
And Sifter,as the Winds giue Benefit,
And Conuoy is affiftant; doe not fleepe,
But let me heare from you.

Ophel. Doe you doubt that?

Laer. For *Hamlet*,and the trifling of his fauours,
Hold it a fafhion and a toy in Bloud;
A Violet in the youth of Primy Nature;
Froward,not permanent; fweer not lafting
The fuppliance of a minute? No more.

Ophel. No more but fo.

Laer. Thinke it no more :
For nature creffant does not grow alone,
In thewes and Bulke: but as his Temple waxes,
The inward feruice of the Minde and Soule
Growes wide withall. Perhaps he loues you now,
And now no foyle nor cautell doth befmerch
The vertue of his feare : but you muft feare

His

His greatnesse weigh'd, his will is not his owne;
For hee himselfe is subiect to his Birth :
Hee may not, as vnuallued persons doe,
Carue for himselfe ; for, on his choyce depends
The sanctity and health of the weole State.
And therefore must his choyce be circumscrib'd
Vnto the voyce and yeelding of that Body,
Whereof he is the Head. Then if he sayes he loues you,
It fits your wisedome so farre to beleeue it ;
As he in his peculiar Sect and force
May giue his saying deed: which is no further,
Then the maine voyce of *Denmarke* goes withall.
Then weigh what losse your Honour may sustaine,
If with too credent eare you list his Songs ;
Or lose your Heart; or your chast Treasure open
To his vnmastred importunity.
Feare it *Ophelia*, feare it my deare Sister,
And keepe within the reare of your Affection;
Out of the shot and danger of Desire.
The chariest Maid is Prodigall enough,
If she vnmaske her beauty to the Moone :
Vertue it selfe scapes not calumnious stroakes,
The Canker Galls, the Infants of the Spring
Too oft before the buttons be disclos'd,
And in the Morne and liquid dew of Youth,
Contagious blastments are most imminent.
Be wary then, best safety lies in feare;
Youth to it selfe rebels, though none else neere.

  Ophe. I shall th'effect of this good Lesson keepe,
As watchmen to my heart : but good my Brother
Doe not as some vngracious Pastors doe,
Shew me the steepe and thorny way to Heauen;
Whilst like a puft and recklesse Libertine
Himselfe, the Primrose path of dalliance treads,
And reaks not his owne reade.

  Laer. Oh, feare me not.

Enter Polonius.

I stay too long ; but here my Father comes :
A double blessing is a double grace;
Occasion smiles vpon a second leaue.

  Polon. Yet heere *Laertes?* Aboord, aboord for shame,
The winde sits in the shoulder of your saile,
And you are staid for there : my blessing with you;
And these few Precepts in thy memory,
See thou Character. Giue thy thoughts no tongue,
Nor any vnproportion'd thought his Act :
Be thou familiar; but by no meanes vulgar:
The friends thou hast, and their adoption tride,
Grapple them to thy Soule, with hoopes of Steele :
But doe not dull thy palme, with entertainment
Of each vnhatch't, vnfledg'd Comrade. Beware
Of entrance to a quarrell : but being in
Bear't that th'opposed may beware of thee.
Giue euery man thine eare; but few thy voyce:
Take each mans censure; but reserue thy iudgement :
Costly thy habit as thy purse can buy ;
But not exprest in fancie; rich, not gawdie:
For the Apparell oft proclaimes the man.
And they in France of the best ranck and station,
Are of a most select and generous cheff in that.
Neither a borrower, nor a lender be;
For lone oft loses both it selfe and friend:
And borrowing duls the edge of Husbandry.
This aboue all; to thine owne selfe be true:
And it must follow, as the Night the Day,
Thou canst not then be false to any man.

Farewell: my Blessing season this in thee.
  Laer. Most humbly doe I take my leaue, my Lord.
  Polon. The time inuites you, goe, your seruants tend.
  Laer. Farewell *Ophelia*, and remember well
What I haue said to you.
  Ophe. Tis in my memory lockt,
And you your selfe shall keepe the key of it.
  Laer. Farewell.   *Exit Laer.*
  Polon. What ist *Ophelia* he hath said to you?
  Ophe. So please you, somthing touching the L. *Hamlet.*
  Polon. Marry, well bethought:
Tis told me he hath very oft of late
Giuen priuate time to you; and you your selfe
Haue of your audience beene most free and bounteous.
If it be so, as so tis put on me;
And that in way of caution: I must tell you,
You doe not vnderstand your selfe so cleerely,
As it behoues my Daughter, and your Honour.
What is betweene you, giue me vp the truth?
  Ophe. He hath my Lord of late, made many tenders
Of his affection to me.
  Polon. Affection, puh. You speake like a greene Girle,
Vnsifted in such perillous Circumstance.
Doe you beleeue his tenders, as you call them?
  Ophe. I do not know, my Lord, what I should thinke.
  Polon. Marry Ile teach you; thinke your selfe a Baby,
That you haue tane his tenders for true pay,
Which are not starling. Tender your selfe more dearly;
Or not to crack the winde of the poore Phrase,
Roaming it thus, you'l tender me a foole.
  Ophe. My Lord, he hath importun'd me with loue,
In honourable fashion.
  Polon. I, fashion you may call it, go too, go too.
  Ophe. And hath giuen countenance to his speech,
My Lord, with all the vowes of Heauen.
  Polon. I, Springes to catch Woodcocks. I doe know
When the Bloud burnes, how Prodigall the Soule
Giues the tongue vowes: these blazes, Daughter,
Giuing more light then heate; extinct in both,
Euen in their promise, as it is a making;
You must not take for fire. For this time Daughter,
Be somewhat scanter of your Maiden presence;
Set your entreatments at a higher rate,
Then a command to parley. For Lord *Hamlet*,
Beleeue so much in him, that he is young,
And with a larger tether may he walke,
Then may be giuen you. In few, *Ophelia*,
Doe not beleeue his vowes; for they are Broakers,
Not of the eye, which their Inuestments show :
But meere implorators of vnholy Sutes,
Breathing like sanctified and pious bonds,
The better to beguile. This is for all :
I would not, in plaine tearmes, from this time forth,
Haue you so slander any moment leisure,
As to giue words or talke with the Lord *Hamlet*:
Looke too't, I charge you; come your wayes.
  Ophe. I shall obey my Lord.   *Exeunt.*

Enter Hamlet, Horatio, Marcellus.

  Ham. The Ayre bites shrewdly : is it very cold?
  Hor. It is a nipping and an eager ayre.
  Ham. What hower now?
  Hor. I thinke it lacks of twelue.
  Mar. No, it is strooke.   (season,
  Hor. Indeed I heard it not : then it drawes neere the
Wherein the Spirit held his wont to walke.

         What

What does this meane my Lord ?   (rouse,

Ham. The King doth wake to night, and takes his
Keepes waffels and the fwaggering vpfpring reeles,
And as he dreines his draughts of Renifh downe,
The kettle Drum and Trumpet thus bray out
The triumph of his Pledge.

Horat. Is it a cuftome ?

Ham. I marry ift;
And to my mind, though I am natiue heere,
And to the manner borne: It is a Cuftome
More honour'd in the breach, then the obferuance.

Enter Ghoft.

Hor. Looke my Lord, it comes.

Ham. Angels and Minifters of Grace defend vs:
Be thou a Spirit of health, or Goblin damn'd,
Bring with thee ayres from Heauen, or blafts from Hell,
Be thy euents wicked or charitable,
Thou com'ft in fuch a queftionable fhape
That I will fpeake to thee. Ile call thee *Hamlet*,
King, Father, Royall Dane : Oh, oh, anfwer me,
Let me not burft in Ignorance; but tell
Why thy Canoniz'd bones Hearfed in death,
Haue burft their cerments; why the Sepulcher
Wherein we faw thee quietly enurn'd,
Hath op'd his ponderous and Marble iawes,
To caft thee vp againe ? What may this meane?
That thou dead Coarfe againe in compleat fteele,
Reuifits thus the glimpfes of the Moone,
Making Night hidious? And we fooles of Nature,
So horridly to fhake our difpofition,
With thoughts beyond thee; reaches of our Soules,
Say, why is this ? wherefore ? what fhould we doe ?

Ghoft beckens Hamlet.

Hor. It beckons you to goe away with it,
As if it fome impartment did defire
To you alone.

Mar. Looke with what courteous action
It wafts you to a more remoued ground :
But doe not goe with it.

Hor. No, by no meanes.

Ham. It will not fpeake: then will I follow it.

Hor. Doe not my Lord.

Ham. Why, what fhould be the feare ?
I doe not fet my life at a pins fee;
And for my Soule, what can it doe to that ?
Being a thing immortall as it felfe :
It waues me forth againe; Ile follow it.

Hor. What if it tempt you toward the Floud my Lord?
Or to the dreadfull Sonnet of the Cliffe,
That beetles o're his bafe into the Sea,
And there affumes fome other horrible forme,
Which might depriue your Soueraignty of Reafon,
And draw you into madneffe thinke of it?

Ham. It wafts me ftill : goe on, Ile follow thee.

Mar. You fhall not goe my Lord.

Ham. Hold off your hand.

Hor. Be rul'd, you fhall not goe.

Ham. My fate cries out,
And makes each petty Artire in this body,
As hardy as the Nemian Lions nerue :
Still am I cal'd ? Vnhand me Gentlemen :
By Heau'n, Ile make a Ghoft of him that lets me :
I fay away, goe on, Ile follow thee.

Exeunt Ghoft & Hamlet.

Hor. He waxes defperate with imagination.

Mar. Let's follow; 'tis not fit thus to obey him.

Hor. Haue after, to what iffue will this come ?

Mar. Something is rotten in the State of Denmarke.

Hor. Heauen will direct it.

Mar. Nay, let's follow him.   *Exeunt.*

Enter Ghoft and Hamlet.   (ther.

Ham. Where wilt thou lead me? fpeak; Ile go no fur-

Gho. Marke me.

Ham. I will.

Gho. My hower is almoft come,
When I to fulphurous and tormenting Flames
Muft render vp my felfe.

Ham. Alas poore Ghoft.

Gho. Pitty me not, but lend thy ferious hearing
To what I fhall vnfold.

Ham. Speake, I am bound to heare.

Gho. So art thou to reuenge, when thou fhalt heare.

Ham. What ?

Gho. I am thy Fathers Spirit,
Doom'd for a certaine terme to walke the night;
And for the day confin'd to faft in Fiers,
Till the foule crimes done in my dayes of Nature
Are burnt and purg'd away ? But that I am forbid
To tell the fecrets of my Prifon-Houfe;
I could a Tale vnfold, whofe lighteft word
Would harrow vp thy foule, freeze thy young blood,
Make thy two eyes like Starres, ftart from their Spheres,
Thy knotty and combined locks to part,
And each particular haire to ftand an end,
Like Quilles vpon the fretfull Porpentine :
But this eternall blafon muft not be
To eares of flefh and bloud; lift *Hamlet*, oh lift,
If thou didft euer thy deare Father loue.

Ham. Oh Heauen!

Gho. Reuenge his foule and moft vnnaturall Murther.

Ham. Murther?

Ghoft. Murther moft foule, as in the beft it is ;
But this moft foule, ftrange, and vnnaturall.

Ham. Haft, haft me to know it,
That with wings as fwift
As meditation, or the thoughts of Loue,
May fweepe to my Reuenge.

Ghoft. I finde thee apt,
And duller fhould'ft thou be then the fat weede
That rots it felfe in eafe, on Lethe Wharfe,
Would'ft thou not ftirre in this. Now *Hamlet* heare :
It's giuen out, that fleeping in mine Orchard,
A Serpent ftung me : fo the whole eare of Denmarke,
Is by a forged proceffe of my death
Rankly abus'd : But know thou Noble youth,
The Serpent that did fting thy Fathers life,
Now weares his Crowne.

Ham. O my Propheticke foule : mine Vncle ?

Ghoft. I that inceftuous, that adulterate Beaft
With witchcraft of his wits, hath Traitorous guifts.
Oh wicked Wit, and Gifts, that haue the power
So to feduce ? Won to to this fhamefull Luft
The will of my moft feeming vertuous Queene:
Oh *Hamlet*, what a falling off was there,
From me, whofe loue was of that dignity,
That it went hand in hand, euen with the Vow
I made to her in Marriage; and to decline
Vpon a wretch, whofe Naturall gifts were poore
To thofe of mine. But Vertue, as it neuer wil be moued,
Though Lewdneffe court it in a fhape of Heauen :
So Luft, though to a radiant Angell link'd,
Will fate it felfe in a Celeftiall bed, & prey on Garbage.

O o   But

But soft,me thinkes I sent the Mornings Ayre;
Briefe let me be : Sleeping within mine Orchard,
My custome alwayes in the afternoone;
Vpon my secure hower thy Vncle stole
With iuyce of cursed Hebenon in a Violl,
And in the Porches of mine eares did poure
The leaperous Distilment; whose effect
Holds such an enmity with bloud of Man,
That swift as Quick-siluer,it courses through
The naturall Gates and Allies of the Body ;
And with a sodaine vigour it doth posset
And curd, like Aygre droppings into Milke,
The thin and wholsome blood : so did it mine ;
And a most instant Tetter bak'd about,
Most Lazar-like, with vile and loathsome crust,
All my smooth Body.
Thus was I, sleeping, by a Brothers hand,
Of Life,of Crowne, and Queene at once dispatcht ;
Cut off euen in the Blossomes of my Sinne,
Vnhouzzled, disappointed, vnnaneld,
No reckoning made,but sent to my account
With all my imperfections on my head;
Oh horrible,Oh horrible, most horrible:
If thou hast nature in thee beare it not;
Let not the Royall Bed of Denmarke be
A Couch for Luxury and damned Incest.
But howsoeuer thou pursuest this Act,
Taint not thy mind ; nor let thy Soule contriue
Against thy Mother ought; leaue her to heauen ,
And to those Thornes that in her bosome lodge,
To pricke and sting her. Fare thee well at once;
The Glow-worme showes the Matine to be neere,
And gins to pale his vneffectuall Fire:
Adue,adue,*Hamlet* : remember me.   *Exit.*
   Ham Oh all you host of Heauen ! Oh Earth; what els?
And shall I couple Hell ? Oh fie : hold my heart;
And you my sinnewes,grow not instant Old;
But beare me stiffely vp : Remember thee ?
I, thou poore Ghost , while memory holds a seate
In this distracted Globe : Remember thee ?
Yea,from the Table of my Memory,
Ile wipe away all triuiall fond Records,
All sawes of Bookes,all formes, all presures past,
That youth and obseruation coppied there;
And thy Commandment all alone shall liue
Within the Booke and Volume of my Braine,
Vnmixt with baser matter; yes, yes, by Heauen :
Oh most pernicious woman !
Oh Villaine, Villaine, smiling damned Villaine !
My Tables,my Tables; meet it is I set it downe,
That one may smile,and smile and be a Villaine;
At least I'm sure it may be so in Denmarke ;
So Vnckle there you are : now to my word;
It is; Adue,Adue, Remember me: I haue sworn't.
   Hor. & Mar.within. My Lord,my Lord.
      Enter Horatio and Marcellus.
   Mar. Lord *Hamlet.*
   Hor. Heauen secure him.
   Mar. So be it.
   Hor. Illo, ho,ho, my Lord.
   Ham. Hillo, ho,ho,boy; come bird,come.
   Mar. How ist't my Noble Lord?
   Hor. What newes, my Lord?
   Ham. Oh wonderfull!
   Hor. Good my Lord tell it.
   Ham. No you'l reueale it.

   Hor. Not I, my Lord, by Heauen.
   Mar. Nor I , my Lord.   (think it?
   Ham. How say you then, would heart of man once
But you'l be secret?
   Both. I, by Heau'n, my Lord.
   Ham. There's nere a villaine dwelling in all Denmarke
But hee's an arrant knaue.
   Hor. There needs no Ghost my Lord, come from the
Graue,to tell vs this.
   Ham. Why right,you are i'th' right;
And so, without more circumstance at all,
I hold it fit that we shake hands,and part:
You,as your busines and desires shall point you :
For euery man ha's businesse and desire,
Such as it is : and for mine owne poore part,
Looke you, Ile goe pray.
   Hor. These are but wild and hurling words,my Lord.
   Ham. I'm sorry they offend you heartily :
Yes faith,heartily.
   Hor. There's no offence my Lord.
   Ham. Yes, by Saint *Patricke*,but there is my Lord,
And much offence too, touching this Vision heere :
It is an honest Ghost, that let me tell you :
For your desire to know what is betweene vs,
O'remaster't as you may. And now good friends,
As you are Friends,Schollers and Soldiers,
Giue me one poore request.
   Hor. What is't my Lord? we will.
   Ham Neuer make known what you haue seen to night.
   Both. My Lord,we will not.
   Ham Nay, but swear't.
   Hor. Infaith my Lord, not I.
   Mar. Nor I my Lord : in faith.
   Ham. Vpon my sword.
   Marcell. We haue sworne my Lord already.
   Ham Indeed,vpon my sword,Indeed.
   Gho. Sweare.   *Ghost cries vnder the Stage.*
   Ham. Ah ha boy,sayest thou so. Art thou there true-
penny ? Come one you here this fellow in the selleredge
Consent to sweare.
   Hor. Propose the Oath my Lord.
   Ham. Neuer to speake of this that you haue seene.
Sweare by my sword.
   Gho. Sweare.
   Ham. Hic & vbique? Then wee'l shift for grownd,
Come hither Gentlemen,
And lay your hands againe vpon my sword,
Neuer to speake of this that you haue heard:
Sweare by my Sword.
   Gho. Sweare.   (fast?
   Ham. Well said old Mole,can'st worke i'th' ground so
A worthy Pioner,once more remoue good friends.
   Hor. Oh day and night:but this is wondrous strange.
   Ham. And therefore as a stranger giue it welcome.
There are more things in Heauen and Earth, *Horatio*,
Then are dream't of in our Philosophy But come,
Here as before, neuer so helpe you mercy,
How strange or odde so ere I beare my selfe;
(As I perchance heereafter shall thinke meet
To put an Anticke disposition on :)
That you at such time seeing me, neuer shall
With Armes encombred thus, or thus, head shake;
Or by pronouncing of some doubtfull Phrase;
As well,we know,or we could and if we would,
Or if we list to speake ; or there be and if there might,
Or such ambiguous giuing out to note,
                          That

That you know ought of me; this not to doe :
So grace and mercy at your moſt neede helpe you :
Sweare.

    Ghoſt. Sweare.

    Ham. Reſt, reſt perturbed Spirit: ſo Gentlemen,
With all my loue I doe commend me to you ;
And what ſo poore a man as *Hamlet* is,
May doe t'expreſſe his loue and friending to you,
Godwilling ſhall not lacke : let vs goe in together,
And ſtill your fingers on your lippes I pray,
The time is out of ioynt : Oh curſed ſpight,
That euer I was borne to ſet it right.
Nay, come let's goe together.   *Exeunt.*

Actus Secundus.

    Enter Polonius, and Reynoldo.

    Polon. Giue him his money, and theſe notes *Reynoldo.*
    Reynol. I will my Lord.
    Polon. You ſhall doe maruels wiſely: good *Reynoldo,*
Before you viſite him you make inquiry
Of his behauiour.
    Reynol. My Lord, I did intend it.
    Polon. Marry, well ſaid ;
Very well ſaid. Looke you Sir,
Enquire me firſt what Danskers are in Paris;
And how, and who; what meanes; and where they keepe:
What company, at what expence : and finding
By this encompaſſement and drift of queſtion,
That they doe know my ſonne : Come you more neerer
Then your particular demands will touch it,
Take you as 'twere ſome diſtant knowledge of him,
And thus I know his father and his friends,
And in part him. Doe you marke this *Reynoldo?*
    Reynol. I, very well my Lord.
    Polon. And in part him, but you may ſay not well;
But if't be hee I meane, hees very wilde;
Addicted ſo and ſo; and there put on him
What forgeries you pleaſe : marry, none ſo ranke,
As may diſhonour him ; take heed of that :
But Sir, ſuch wanton, wild, and vſuall ſlips,
As are Companions noted and moſt knowne
To youth and liberty.
    Reynol. As gaming my Lord.
    Polon. I, or drinking, fencing, ſwearing,
Quarelling, drabbing. You may goe ſo farre.
    Reynol. My Lord that would diſhonour him.
    Polon. Faith no, as you may ſeaſon it in the charge;
You muſt not put another ſcandall on him,
That hee is open to Incontinencie;
That's not my meaning: but breath his faults ſo quaintly,
That they may ſeeme the taints of liberty;
The flaſh and out-breake of a fiery minde,
A ſauagenes in vnreclaim'd bloud of generall aſſault.
    Reynol. But my good Lord.
    Polon. Wherefore ſhould you doe this?
    Reynol. I my Lord, I would know that.
    Polon. Marry Sir, heere's my drift,
And I belieue it is a fetch of warrant:
You laying theſe ſlight ſulleyes on my Sonne,
As 'twere a thing a little ſoil'd i'th' working :   (found,
Marke you your party in conuerſe ; him you would
Hauing euer ſeene. In the prenominate crimes,

The youth you breath of guilty, be aſſur'd
He cloſes with you in this conſequence:
Good ſir, or ſo, or friend, or Gentleman.
According to the Phraſe and the Addition,
Of man and Country.
    Reynol. Very good my Lord.
    Polon. And then Sir does he this ?
He does : what was I about to ſay?
I was about to ſay ſomthing : where did I leaue ?
    Reynol. At cloſes in the conſequence :
At friend, or ſo, and Gentleman.
    Polon. At cloſes in the conſequence, I marry,
He cloſes with you thus. I know the Gentleman,
I ſaw him yeſterday, or tother day;
Or then or then, with ſuch and ſuch; and as you ſay,
There was he gaming, there o're-tooke in's Rouſe,
There falling out at Tennis ; or perchance,
I ſaw him enter ſuch a houſe of ſaile;
Videlicet, a Brothell, or ſo forth. See you now;
Your bait of falſhood, takes this Cape of truth ;
And thus doe we of wiſedome and of reach
With windleſſes, and with aſſaies of Bias,
By indirections finde directions out :
So by my former Lecture and aduice
Shall you my Sonne; you haue me, haue you not ?
    Reynol. My Lord I haue.
    Polon. God buy you; fare you well.
    Reynol. Good my Lord.
    Polon. Obſerue his inclination in your ſelfe.
    Reynol. I ſhall my Lord.
    Polon. And let him plye his Muſicke.
    Reynol. Well, my Lord.   *Exit.*

    Enter Ophelia.

    Polon. Farewell :
How now *Ophelia,* what's the matter?
    Ophe. Alas my Lord, I haue beene ſo affrighted.
    Polon. With what, in the name of Heauen ?
    Ophe. My Lord, as I was ſowing in my Chamber,
Lord *Hamlet* with his doublet all vnbrac'd,
No hat vpon his head, his ſtockings foul'd,
Vngartred, and downe giued to his Anckle,
Pale as his ſhirt, his knees knocking each other,
And with a looke ſo pitious in purport,
As if he had been looſed out of hell,
To ſpeake of horrors : he comes before me.
    Polon. Mad for thy Loue ?
    Ophe. My Lord, I doe not know: but truly I do feare it.
    Polon. What ſaid he?
    Ophe. He tooke me by the wriſt, and held me hard ;
Then goes he to the length of all his arme;
And with his other hand thus o're his brow,
He fals to ſuch peruſall of my face,
As he would draw it. Long ſtaid he ſo,
At laſt, a little ſhaking of mine Arme:
And thrice his head thus wauing vp and downe;
He rais'd a ſigh, ſo pittious and profound,
That it did ſeeme to ſhatter all his bulke,
And end his being. That done, he lets me goe,
And with his head ouer his ſhoulders turn'd,
He ſeem'd to finde his way without his eyes,
For out a dores he went without their helpe;
And to the laſt, bended their light on me.
    Polon. Goe with me, I will goe ſeeke the King,
This is the very extaſie of Loue,
Whoſe violent property foredoes it ſelfe,

    And

And leads the will to desperate Vndertakings,
As oft as any passion vnder Heauen,
That does afflict our Natures. I am sorrie,
What haue you giuen him any hard words of late?

Ophe. No my good Lord : but as you did command,
I did repell his Letters, and deny'de
His accesse to me.

Pol. That hath made him mad.
I am sorrie that with better speed and iudgement
I had not quoted him. I feare he did but trifle,
And meant to wracke thee : but beshrew my iealousie:
It seemes it is as proper to our Age,
To cast beyond our selues in our Opinions,
As it is common for the yonger sort
To lacke discretion. Come, go we to the King,
This must be knowne, w being kept close might moue
More greefe to hide, then hate to vtter loue.   *Exeunt.*

Scena Secunda.

*Enter King, Queene, Rosincrane, and Guilden-
sterne Cum alijs.*

King. Welcome deere *Rosincrance* and *Guildensterne.*
Moreouer, that we much did long to see you,
The neede we haue to vse you, did prouoke
Our hastie sending. Something haue you heard
Of *Hamlets* transformation : so I call it,
Since not th'exterior, nor the inward man
Resembles that it was. What it should bee
More then his Fathers death, that thus hath put him
So much from th'vnderstanding of himselfe,
I cannot deeme of. I intreat you both,
That being of so young dayes brought vp with him :
And since so Neighbour'd to his youth, and humour,
That you vouchsafe your rest heere in our Court
Some little time : so by your Companies
To draw him on to pleasures, and to gather
So much as from Occasions you may gleane,
That open'd lies within our remedie.

Qu. Good Gentlemen, he hath much talk'd of you,
And sure I am, two men there are not liuing,
To whom he more adheres. If it will please you
To shew vs so much Gentrie, and good will,
As to expend your time with vs a-while,
For the supply and profit of our Hope,
Your Visitation shall receiue such thankes
As fits a Kings remembrance.

Rosin. Both your Maiesties
Might by the Soueraigne power you haue of vs,
Put your dread pleasures, more into Command
Then to Entreatie.

Guil. We both obey,
And here giue vp our selues, in the full bent,
To lay our Seruices freely at your feete,
To be commanded.

King. Thankes *Rosincrance,* and gentle *Guildensterne.*
Qu. Thankes *Guildensterno* and gentle *Rosincrance.*
And I beseech you instantly to visit
My too much changed Sonne.
Go some of ye,
And bring the Gentlemen where *Hamlet* is.

Guil. Heauens make our presence and our practises
Pleasant and helpfull to him.   *Exit.*

Queene. Amen.

Enter Polonius.

Pol. Th'Ambassadors from Norwey, my good Lord,
Are ioyfully return'd.

King. Thou still hast bin the Father of good Newes.

Pol. Haue I, my Lord ? Assure you, my good Liege,
I hold my dutie, as I hold my Soule,
Both to my God, one to my gracious King :
And I do thinke, or else this braine of mine
Hunts not the traile of Policie, so sure
As I haue vs'd to do : that I haue found
The very cause of *Hamlets* Lunacie.

King. Oh speake of that, that I do long to heare.

Pol. Giue first admittance to th'Ambassadors,
My Newes shall be the Newes to that great Feast.

King. Thy selfe do grace to them, and bring them in.
He tels me my sweet Queene, that he hath found
The head and fourse of all your Sonnes distemper.

Qu. I doubt it is no other, but the maine,
His Fathers death, and our o're-hasty Marriage.

Enter Polonius, Voltumand, and Cornelius.

King. Well, we shall sift him. Welcome good Frends:
Say *Voltumand,* what from our Brother Norwey ?

Volt. Most faire returne of Greetings, and Desires.
Vpon our first, he sent out to suppresse
His Nephewes Leuies, which to him appear'd
To be a preparation 'gainst the Poleak :
But better look'd into, he truly found
It was against your Highnesse, whereat greeued,]
That so his Sicknesse, Age, and Impotence
Was falsely borne in hand, sends out Arrests
On *Fortinbras,* which he (in breefe) obeyes,
Receiues rebuke from Norwey: and in fine,
Makes Vow before his Vnkle, neuer more
To giue th'assay of Armes against your Maiestie.
Whereon old Norwey, ouercome with ioy,
Giues him three thousand Crownes in Annuall Fee,
And his Commission to imploy those Soldiers
So leuied as before, against the Poleak :
With an intreaty heerein further shewne,
That it might please you to giue quiet passe
Through your Dominions, for his Enterprize,
On such regards of safety and allowance,
As therein are set downe.

King. It likes vs well :
And at our more consider'd time wee'l read,
Answer, and thinke vpon this Businesse.
Meane time we thanke you, for your well-tooke Labour.
Go to your rest, at night wee'l Feast together.
Most welcome home.   *Exit Ambass.*

Pol. This businesse is very well ended.
My Liege, and Madam, to expostulate
What Maiestie should be, what Dutie is,
Why day is day ; night, night ; and time is time,
Were nothing but to waste Night, Day and Time.
Therefore, since Breuitie is the Soule of Wit,
And tediousnesse, the limbes and outward flourishes,
I will be breefe. Your Noble Sonne is mad :
Mad call I it ; for to define true Madnesse,
What is't, but to be nothing else but mad.
But let that go.

Qu. More matter, with lesse Art.

Pol. Madam, I sweare I vse no Art at all :
That he is mad, 'tis true : 'Tis true 'tis pittie,
And pittie it is true : A foolish figure,
But farewell it : for I will vse no Art.

Mad let vs grant him then : and now remaines
That we finde out the cause of this effect,
Or rather say, the cause of this defect ;
For this effect defectiue, comes by cause,
Thus it remaines, and the remainder thus. *Perpend*,
I haue a daughter : haue, whil'st she is mine,
Who in her Dutie and Obedience, marke,
Hath giuen me this : now gather, and surmise.

    The Letter.
To the *Celestiall*, and my *Soules Idoll*, *the most beautified O-*
phelia.

That's an ill Phrase, a vilde Phrase, beautified is a vilde
Phrase : but you shall heare these in her excellent white
bosome, these.

  Qu. Came this from *Hamlet* to her.
  Pol. Good Madam stay awhile, I will be faithfull.
Doubt thou, the Starres are fire,
Doubt, that the Sunne doth moue :
Doubt Truth to be a Lier,
But neuer Doubt, I loue.
O deere *Ophelia*, I am ill at these Numbers : I haue not Art to
reckon my grones ; but that I loue thee best, oh most Best be-
leeue it. *Adieu.*

    Thine euermore most deere Lady, whilst this
        Machine is to him, Hamlet.

This in Obedience hath my daughter shew'd me :
And more aboue hath his soliciting,
As they fell out by Time, by Meanes, and Place,
All giuen to mine eare.

  King. But how hath she receiu'd his Loue?
  Pol. What do you thinke of me?
  King. As of a man, faithfull and Honourable.
  Pol. I wold faine proue so. But what might you think?
When I had seene this hot loue on the wing,
As I perceiued it, I must tell you that
Before my Daughter told me, what might you
Or my deere Maiestie your Queene heere, think,
If I had playd the Deske or Table-booke,
Or giuen my heart a winking, mute and dumbe,
Or look'd vpon this Loue, with idle sight,
What might you thinke? No, I went round to worke,
And (my yong Mistris) thus I did bespeake
Lord *Hamlet* is a Prince out of thy Starre,
This must not be : and then, I Precepts gaue her,
That she should locke her selfe from his Resort,
Admit no Messengers, receiue no Tokens :
Which done, she tooke the Fruites of my Aduice,
And he repulsed. A short Tale to make,
Fell into a Sadnesse, then into a Fast,
Thence to a Watch, thence into a Weaknesse,
Thence to a Lightnesse, and by this declension
Into the Madnesse whereon now he raues,
And all we waile for.

  King. Do you thinke 'tis this?
  Qu. It may be very likely.
  Pol. Hath there bene such a time, I'de faine know that,
That I haue positiuely said, 'tis so,
When it prou'd otherwise?
  King. Not that I know.
  Pol. Take this from this ; if this be otherwise,
If Circumstances leade me, I will finde
Where truth is hid, though it were hid indeede
Within the Center.
  King. How may we try it further?
  Pol. You know sometimes
He walkes foure houres together, heere

In the Lobby.
  Qu. So he ha's indeed.
  Pol. At such a time Ile loose my Daughter to him,
Be you and I behinde an Arras then,
Marke the encounter : If he loue her not,
And be not from his reason falne thereon ;
Let me be no Assistant for a State,
And keepe a Farme and Carters.
  King. We will try it.

    Enter Hamlet reading on a Booke.

  Qu. But looke where sadly the poore wretch
Comes reading.
  Pol. Away I do beseech you, both away,
Ile boord him presently.   *Exit King & Queen.*
Oh giue me leaue. How does my good Lord *Hamlet?*
  Ham. Well, God-a-mercy.
  Pol. Do you know me, my Lord?
  Ham. Excellent, excellent well : y'are a Fishmonger.
  Pol. Not I my Lord.
  Ham. Then I would you were so honest a man.
  Pol. Honest, my Lord?
  Ham. I sir, to be honest as this world goes, is to bee
one man pick'd out of two thousand.
  Pol. That's very true, my Lord.
  Ham. For if the Sun breed Magots in a dead dogge,
being a good kissing Carrion————
Haue you a daughter?
  Pol. I haue my Lord.
  Ham. Let her not walke i'th'Sunne : Conception is a
blessing, but not as your daughter may conceiue, Friend
looke too't.
  Pol. How say you by that? Still harping on my daugh-
ter : yet he knew me not at first ; he said I was a Fishmon-
ger : he is farre gone, farre gone : and truly in my youth,
I suffred much extreamity for loue : very neere this. Ile
speake to him againe. What do you read my Lord?
  Ham. Words, words, words.
  Pol. What is the matter, my Lord?
  Ham. Betweene who?
  Pol. I meane the matter you meane, my Lord.
  Ham. Slanders Sir : for the Satyricall slaue saies here,
that old men haue gray Beards ; that their faces are wrin-
kled ; their eyes purging thicke Amber, or Plum-Tree
Gumme : and that they haue a plentifull locke of Wit,
together with weake Hammes. All which Sir, though I
most powerfully, and potently beleeue ; yet I holde it
not Honestie to haue it thus set downe : For you your
selfe Sir, should be old as I am, if like a Crab you could
go backward.
  Pol. Though this be madnesse,
Yet there is Method in't : will you walke
Out of the ayre my Lord?
  Ham. Into my Graue?
  Pol. Indeed that is out o'th'Ayre :
How pregnant (sometimes) his Replies are?
A happinesse,
That often Madnesse hits on,
Which Reason and Sanitie could not
So prosperously be deliuer'd of.
I will leaue him,
And sodainely contriue the meanes of meeting
Betweene him, and my daughter.
My Honourable Lord, I will most humbly
Take my leaue of you.

Ham. You cannot Sir take from me any thing, that I will more willingly part withall, except my life, my life.

Polon. Fare you well my Lord.

Ham. These tedious old fooles.

Polon. You goe to seeke my Lord *Hamlet*; there hee is.

Enter Rosincran and Guildensterne.

Rosin. God saue you Sir.

Guild. Mine honour'd Lord?

Rosin. My most deare Lord?

Ham. My excellent good friends? How do'st thou *Guildensterne*? Oh, *Rosincrane*; good Lads: How doe ye both?

Rosin. As the indifferent Children of the earth.

Guild. Happy, in that we are not ouer-happy: on Fortunes Cap, we are not the very Button.

Ham. Nor the Soales of her Shoo?

Rosin. Neither my Lord.

Ham. Then you liue about her waste, or in the middle of her fauour?

Guil. Faith, her priuates, we.

Ham. In the secret parts of Fortune? Oh, most true: she is a Strumpet. What's the newes?

Rosin. None my Lord; but that the World's growne honest.

Ham. Then is Doomesday neere: But your newes is not true. Let me question more in particular: what haue you my good friends, deserued at the hands of Fortune, that she sends you to Prison hither?

Guil. Prison, my Lord?

Ham. Denmark's a Prison.

Rosin. Then is the World one.

Ham. A goodly one, in which there are many Confines, Wards, and Dungeons; *Denmarke* being one o'th' worst.

Rosin. We thinke not so my Lord.

Ham. Why then 'tis none to you; for there is nothing either good or bad, but thinking makes it so: to me it is a prison.

Rosin. Why then your Ambition makes it one: 'tis too narrow for your minde.

Ham. O God, I could be bounded in a nutshell, and count my selfe a King of infinite space; were it not that I haue bad dreames.

Guil. Which dreames indeed are Ambition: for the very substance of the Ambitious, is meerely the shadow of a Dreame.

Ham. A dreame it selfe is but a shadow.

Rosin. Truely, and I hold Ambition of so ayry and light a quality, that it is but a shadowes shadow.

Ham. Then are our Beggers bodies; and our Monarchs and out-stretcht Heroes the Beggers Shadowes: shall wee to th' Court: for, by my fey I cannot reason?

Both. Wee'l wait vpon you.

Ham. No such matter. I will not sort you with the rest of my seruants: for to speake to you like an honest man: I am most dreadfully attended; but in the beaten way of friendship, What make you at *Elsonower*?

Rosin. To visit you my Lord, no other occasion.

Ham. Begger that I am, I am euen poore in thankes; but I thanke you: and sure deare friends my thanks are too deare a halfepeny; were you not sent for? Is it your owne inclining? Is it a free visitation? Come, deale iustly with me: come, come; nay speake.

Guil. What should we say my Lord?

Ham. Why any thing. But to the purpose; you were sent for; and there is a kinde confession in your lookes; which your modesties haue not craft enough to color, I know the good King & Queene haue sent for you.

Rosin. To what end my Lord?

Ham. That you must teach me: but let mee coniure you by the rights of our fellowship, by the consonancy of our youth, by the Obligation of our euer-preserued loue, and by what more deare, a better proposer could charge you withall; be euen and direct with me, whether you were sent for or no.

Rosin. What say you?

Ham. Nay then I haue an eye of you: if you loue me hold not off.

Guil. My Lord, we were sent for.

Ham. I will tell you why; so shall my anticipation preuent your discouery of your secricie to the King and Queene: moult no feather, I haue of late, but wherefore I know not, lost all my mirth, forgone all custome of exercise; and indeed, it goes so heauenly with my disposition; that this goodly frame the Earth, seemes to me a sterrill Promontory; this most excellent Canopy the Ayre, look you, this braue ore-hanging, this Maiesticall Roofe, fretted with golden fire: why, it appeares no other thing to mee, then a foule and pestilent congregation of vapours. What a piece of worke is a man! how Noble in Reason? how infinite in faculty? in forme and mouing how expresse and admirable? in Action, how like an Angel? in apprehension, how like a God? the beauty of the world, the Parragon of Animals; and yet to me, what is this Quintessence of Dust? Man delights not me; no, nor Woman neither; though by your smiling you seeme to say so.

Rosin. My Lord, there was no such stuffe in my thoughts.

Ham. Why did you laugh, when I said, Man delights not me?

Rosin. To thinke, my Lord, if you delight not in Man, what Lenton entertainment the Players shall receiue from you: wee coated them on the way, and hither are they comming to offer you Seruice.

Ham. He that playes the King shall be welcome; his Maiesty shall haue Tribute of mee: the aduenturous Knight shal vse his Foyle and Target: the Louer shall not sigh *gratis*, the humorous man shall end his part in peace: the Clowne shall make those laugh whose lungs are tickled a'th' sere: and the Lady shall say her minde freely; or the blanke Verse shall halt for't: what Players are they?

Rosin. Euen those you were wont to take delight in the Tragedians of the City.

Ham. How chances it they trauaile? their residence both in reputation and profit was better both wayes.

Rosin. I thinke their Inhibition comes by the meanes of the late Innouation?

Ham. Doe they hold the same estimation they did when I was in the City? Are they so follow'd?

Rosin. No indeed, they are not.

Ham. How comes it? doe they grow rusty?

Rosin. Nay, their indeauour keepes in the wonted pace; But there is Sir an ayrie of Children, little Yases, that crye out on the top of question; and are most tyrannically clap't for't: these are now the fashi-

fashion, and so be-ratled the common Stages (so they call them) that many wearing Rapiers, are affraide of Goose-quils, and dare scarse come thither.

Ham. What are they Children? Who maintains 'em? How are they escoted ? Will they pursue the Quality no longer then they can sing ? Will they not say afterwards if they should grow themselues to common Players (as it is like most if their meanes are no better) their Writers do them wrong, to make them exclaim against their owne Succession.

Rosin. Faith there ha's bene much to do on both sides: and the Nation holds it no sinne, to tarre them to Controuersie. There was for a while, no mony bid for argument, vnlesse the Poet and the Player went to Cuffes in the Question.

Ham. Is't possible ?

Guild. Oh there ha's beene much throwing about of Braines.

Ham. Do the Boyes carry it away ?

Rosin. I that they do my Lord, *Hercules* & his load too.

Ham. It is not strange : for mine Vnckle is King of Denmarke, and those that would make mowes at him while my Father liued; giue twenty, forty, an hundred Ducates a peece, for his picture in Little. There is something in this more then Naturall, if Philosophie could finde it out.

Flourish for the Players.

Guil. There are the Players.

Ham. Gentlemen, you are welcom to *Elsonower*: your hands, come: The appurtenance of Welcome, is Fashion and Ceremony. Let me comply with you in the Garbe, lest my extent to the Players(which I tell you must shew fairely outward)should more appeare like entertainment then yours. You are welcome : but my Vnckle Father, and Aunt Mother are deceiu'd.

Guil. In what my deere Lord ?

Ham. I am but mad North, North-West : when the Winde is Southerly, I know a Hawke from a Handsaw.

Enter Polonius.

Pol. Well be with you Gentlemen.

Ham. Hearke you *Guildensterne*, and you too : at each eare a hearer : that great Baby you see there, is not yet out of his swathing clouts.

Rosin. Happily he's the second time come to them: for they say, an old man is twice a childe.

Ham. I will Prophesie. Hee comes to tell me of the Players. Mark it, you say right Sir : for a Monday morning 'twas so indeed.

Pol. My Lord, I haue Newes to tell you.

Ham. My Lord, I haue Newes to tell you. When *Rossius* an Actor in Rome——

Pol. The Actors are come hither my Lord.

Ham. Buzze, buzze.

Pol. Vpon mine Honor.

Ham. Then can each Actor on his Asse ——

Polon. The best Actors in the world, either for Tragedie, Comedie, Historie, Pastorall : Pastoricall-Comicall-Historicall-Pastorall : Tragicall-Historicall : Tragicall-Comicall-Historicall-Pastorall : Scene indiuible, or Poem vnlimited. *Seneca* cannot be too heauy, nor *Plautus* too light, for the law of Writ, and the Liberty. These are the onely men.

Ham. O *Iephta* Iudge of Israel, what a Treasure had'st thou ?

Pol. What a Treasure had he, my Lord ?

Ham. Why one faire Daughter, and no more,

The which he loued passing well.

Pol. Still on my Daughter.

Ham. Am I not i'th'right old *Iephta* ?

Polon. If you call me *Iephta* my Lord, I haue a daughter that I loue passing well.

Ham. Nay that followes not.

Polon. What followes then, my Lord ?

Ha. Why, As by lot, God wot : and then you know, It came to passe, as most like it was : The first rowe of the *Pons Chanson* will shew you more. For looke where my Abridgements come.

Enter foure or fiue Players.

Y'are welcome Masters, welcome all. I am glad to see thee well : Welcome good Friends. O my olde Friend ? Thy face is valiant since I saw thee last : Com'st thou to beard me in Denmarke ? What, my yong Lady and Mistris? Byrlady your Ladiship is neerer Heauen then when I saw you last, by the altitude of a Choppine. Pray God your voice like a peece of vncurrant Gold be not crack'd within the ring. Masters, you are all welcome: wee'l e'ne to't like French Faulconers, flie at any thing we see: wee'l haue a Speech straight. Come giue vs a tait of your quality : come, a passionate speech.

1. Play. What speech, my Lord ?

Ham. I heard thee speak me a speech once, but it was neuer Acted : or if it was, not aboue once, for the Play I remember pleas'd not the Million, 'twas *Cauiarie* to the Generall : but it was (as I receiu'd it, and others, whose iudgement in such matters, cried in the top of mine) an excellent Play : well digested in the Scœnes, set downe with as much modestie, as cunning. I remember one said there was no Sallets in the lines, to make the matter sauoury; nor no matter in the phrase, that might indite the Author of affectation, but cal'd it an honest method. One cheefe Speech in it, I cheefely lou'd, 'twas *Æneas* Tale to *Dido*, and thereabout of it especially, where he speaks of *Priams* slaughter. If it liue in your memory, begin at this Line, let me see, let me see : The rugged *Pyrrhus* like th'*Hyrcanian* Beast. It is not so : it begins with *Pyrrhus*
The rugged *Pyrrhus*, he whose Sable Armes
Blacke as his purpose, did the night resemble
When he lay couched in the Ominous Horse,
Hath now this dread and blacke Complexion smear'd
With Heraldry more dismall : Head to foote
Now is he to take Geulles, horridly Trick'd
With blood of Fathers, Mothers, Daughters, Sonnes,
Bak'd and impasted with the parching streets,
That lend a tyrannous, and damned light
To their vilde Murthers, roasted in wrath and fire,
And thus o're-sized with coagulate gore,
VVith eyes like Carbuncles, the hellish *Pyrrhus*
Old Grandsire *Priam* seekes.

Pol. Fore God, my Lord, well spoken, with good accent, and good discretion.

1. Player. Anon he findes him,
Striking too short at Greekes. His anticke Sword,
Rebellious to his Arme, lyes where it falles
Repugnant to command : vnequall match,
Pyrrhus at *Priam* driues, in Rage strikes wide :
But with the whiffe and winde of his fell Sword,
Th'vnnerued Father fals. Then senselesse Illium,
Seeming to feele his blow, with flaming top
Stoopes to his Bace, and with a hideous crash
Takes Prisoner *Pyrrhus* eare. For loe, his Sword
Which was declining on the Milkie head
Of Reuerend *Priam*, seem'd i'th'Ayre to sticke :

So as a painted Tyrant *Pyrrhus* stood,
And like a Newtrall to his will and matter, did nothing.
But as we often see against some storme,
A silence in the Heauens, the Racke stand still,
The bold windes speechlesse, and the Orbe below
As hush as death : Anon the dreadfull Thunder
Doth rend the Region. So after *Pyrrhus* pause,
A rowsed Vengeance sets him new a-worke,
And neuer did the Cyclops hammers fall
On Mars his Armours, forg'd for proofe Eterne,
With lesse remorse then *Pyrrhus* bleeding sword
Now falles on *Priam.*
Out, out, thou Strumpet-Fortune, all you Gods,
In generall Synod take away her power :
Breake all the Spokes and Fallies from her wheele,
And boule the round Naue downe the hill of Heauen,
As low as to the Fiends.

Pol. This is too long.

Ham. It shall to'th Barbars, with your beard. Prythee say on : He's for a Iigge, or a tale of Baudry, or hee
sleepes. Say on ; come to *Hecuba.*

1.Play. But who, O who, had seene the inobled Queen.

Ham. The inobled Queene ?

Pol. That's good : Inobled Queene is good.

2.Play. Run bare-foot vp and downe,
Threatning the flame
With Bisson Rheume : A clout about that head,
Where late the Diadem stood, and for a Robe
About her lanke and all ore-teamed Loines,
A blanket in th'Alarum of feare caught vp.
Who this had seene, with tongue in Venome steep'd,
'Gainst Fortunes State, would Treason haue pronounc'd?
But if the Gods themselues did see her then,
When she saw *Pyrrhus* make malicious sport
In mincing with his Sword her Husbands limbes,
The instant Burst of Clamour that she made
(Vnlesse things mortall moue them not at all)
Would haue made milche the Burning eyes of Heauen,
And passion in the Gods.

Pol. Looke where he ha's not turn'd his colour, and
ha's teares in's eyes. Pray you no more.

Ham. 'Tis well, Ile haue thee speake out the rest,
soone. Good my Lord, will you see the Players wel bestow'd. Do ye heare, let them be well vs'd : for they are
the Abstracts and breefe Chronicles of the time. After
your death, you were better haue a bad Epitaph, then
their ill report while you liued.

Pol. My Lord, I will vse them according to their desart.

Ham. Gods bodykins man, better. Vse euerie man
after his desart, and who should scape whipping : vse
them after your own Honor and Dignity. The lesse they
deserue, the more merit is in your bountie. Take them
in.

Pol. Come sirs.   *Exit Polon.*

Ham. Follow him Friends:wee'l heare a play to morrow. Dost thou heare me old Friend, can you play the
murther of *Gonzago* ?

Play. I my Lord.

Ham. Wee'l ha't to morrow night. You could for a
need study a speech of some dosen or sixteene lines,which
I would set downe,and insert in't? Could ye not ?

Play. I my Lord.

Ham. Very well. Follow that Lord, and looke you
mock him not. My good Friends, Ile leaue you til night
you are welcome to *Elsonower* ?

Rosin. Good my Lord.   *Exeunt.*

Manet Hamlet.

Ham. I so, God buy'ye : Now I am alone.
Oh what a Rogue and Pesant slaue am I ?
Is it not monstrous that this Player heere,
But in a Fixion, in a dreame of Passion,
Could force his soule so to his whole conceit,
That from her working, all his visage warm'd;
Teares in his eyes, distraction in's Aspect,
A broken voyce, and his whole Function suiting
With Formes, to his Conceit ? And all for nothing ?
For *Hecuba* ?
What's *Hecuba* to him, or he to *Hecuba,*
That he should weepe for her ? What would he doe,
Had he the Motiue and the Cue for passion
That I haue ? He would drowne the Stage with teares,
And cleaue the generall eare with horrid speech :
Make mad the guilty, and apale the free,
Confound the ignorant, and amaze indeed,
The very faculty of Eyes and Eares. Yet I,
A dull and muddy-metled Rascall, peake
Like Iohn a-dreames, vnpregnant of my cause,
And can say nothing : No, not for a King,
Vpon whose property, and most deere life,
A damn'd defeate was made. Am I a Coward ?
Who calles me Villaine ? breakes my pate a-crosse ?
Pluckes off my Beard, and blowes it in my face?
Tweakes me by'th'Nose? giues me the Lye i'th'Throate,
As deepe as to the Lungs? Who does me this ?
Ha? Why I should take it : for it cannot be,
But I am Pigeon-Liuer'd, and lacke Gall
To make Oppression bitter, or ere this,
I should haue fatted all the Region Kites
With this Slaues Offall, bloudy : a Bawdy villaine,
Remorselesse, Treacherous, Letcherous, kindles villaine !
Oh Vengeance !
Who? What an Asse am I ? I sure, this is most braue,
That I, the Sonne of the Deere murthered,
Prompted to my Reuenge by Heauen, and Hell,
Must (like a Whore) vnpacke my heart with words,
And fall a Cursing like a very Drab,
A Scullion? Fye vpon't : Foh. About my Braine.
I haue heard, that guilty Creatures sitting at a Play,
Haue by the very cunning of the Scoene,
Bene strooke so to the soule, that presently
They haue proclaim'd their Malefactions.
For Murther, though it haue no tongue, will speake
With most myraculous Organ. Ile haue these Players,
Play something like the murder of my Father,
Before mine Vnkle. Ile obserue his lookes,
Ile tent him to the quicke : If he but blench
I know my course. The Spirit that I haue seene
May be the Diuell, and the Diuel hath power
T'assume a pleasing shape, yea and perhaps
Out of my Weaknesse, and my Melancholly,
As he is very potent with such Spirits,
Abuses me to damne me. Ile haue grounds
More Relatiue then this: The Play's the thing,
Wherein Ile catch the Conscience of the King.   *Exit*

Enter King, Queene, Polonius, Ophelia, Ro-
sincrance, Guildenstern, and Lords.

King. And can you by no drift of circumstance
Get from him why he puts on this Confusion :
Grating so harshly all his dayes of quiet

With

With turbulent and dangerous Lunacy.

Rosin. He does confesse he feeles himselfe distracted,
But from what cause he will by no meanes speake.

Guil. Nor do we finde him forward to be sounded,
But with a crafty Madnesse keepes aloose :
When we would bring him on to some Confession
Of his true state.

Qu. Did he receiue you well?

Rosin. Most like a Gentleman.

Guild. But with much forcing of his disposition.

Rosin. Niggard of question, but of our demands
Most free in his reply.

Qu. Did you assay him to any pastime?

Rosin. Madam, it so fell out, that certaine Players
We ore-wrought on the way : of these we told him,
And there did seeme in him a kinde of ioy
To heare of it : They are about the Court,
And (as I thinke) they haue already order
This night to play before him.

Pol. 'Tis most true:
And he beseech'd me to intreate your Maiesties
To heare, and see the matter.

King. With all my heart, and it doth much content me
To heare him so inclin'd. Good Gentlemen,
Giue him a further edge, and driue his purpose on
To these delights.

Rosin. We shall my Lord.   *Exeunt.*

King. Sweet *Gertrude* leaue vs too,
For we haue closely sent for *Hamlet* hither,
That he, as 'twere by accident, may there
Affront *Ophelia.* Her Father, and my selfe (lawful espials)
Will so bestow our selues, that seeing vnseene
We may of their encounter frankely iudge,
And gather by him, as he is behaued,
If't be th'affliction of his loue, or no,
That thus he suffers for.

Qu. I shall obey you,
And for your part *Ophelia,* I do wish
That your good Beauties be the happy cause
Of *Hamlets* wildenesse : so shall I hope your Vertues
Will bring him to his wonted way againe,
To both your Honors.

Ophe. Madam, I wish it may.

Pol. *Ophelia,* walke you heere. Gracious so please ye
We will bestow our selues : Reade on this booke,
That shew of such an exercise may colour
Your lonelinesse. We are oft too blame in this,
'Tis too much prou'd, that with Deuotions visage,
And pious Action, we do surge o're
The diuell himselfe.

King. Oh 'tis true:
How smart a lash that speech doth giue my Conscience?
The Harlots Cheeke beautied with plaist'ring Art
Is not more vgly to the thing that helpes it,
Then is my deede, to my most painted word.
Oh heauie burthen!

Pol. I heare him comming, let's withdraw my Lord.
                                                    Exeunt.

Enter Hamlet.

Ham. To be, or not to be, that is the Question:
Whether 'tis Nobler in the minde to suffer
The Slings and Arrowes of outragious Fortune,
Or to take Armes against a Sea of troubles,
And by opposing end them : to dye, to sleepe
No more ; and by a sleepe, to say we end
The Heart-ake, and the thousand Naturall shockes

That Flesh is heyre too? 'Tis a consummation
Deuoutly to be wish'd. To dye to sleepe,
To sleepe, perchance to Dreame : I, there's the rub,
For in that sleepe of death, what dreames may come,
When we haue shuffel'd off this mortall coile,
Must giue vs pawse. There's the respect
That makes Calamity of so long life :
For who would beare the Whips and Scornes of time,
The Oppressors wrong, the poore mans Contumely,
The pangs of dispriz'd Loue, the Lawes delay,
The insolence of Office, and the Spurnes
That patient merit of the vnworthy takes,
When he himselfe might his *Quietus* make
With a bare Bodkin? Who would these Fardles beare
To grunt and sweat vnder a weary life,
But that the dread of something after death,
The vndiscouered Countrey, from whose Borne
No Traueller returnes, Puzels the will,
And makes vs rather beare those illes we haue,
Then flye to others that we know not of.
Thus Conscience does make Cowards of vs all,
And thus the Natiue hew of Resolution
Is sicklied o're, with the pale cast of Thought,
And enterprizes of great pith and moment,
With this regard their Currants turne away,
And loose the name of Action. Soft you now,
The faire *Ophelia?* Nimph, in thy Orizons
Be all my sinnes remembred.

Ophe. Good my Lord,
How does your Honor for this many a day?

Ham. I humbly thanke you : well, well, well.

Ophe. My Lord, I haue Remembrances of yours,
That I haue longed long to re-deliuer.
I pray you now, receiue them.

Ham. No, no, I neuer gaue you ought.

Ophe. My honor'd Lord, I know right well you did,
And with them words of so sweet breath compos'd,
As made the things more rich, then perfume left :
Take these againe, for to the Noble minde
Rich gifts wax poore, when giuers proue vnkinde.
There my Lord.

Ham. Ha, ha : Are you honest?

Ophe. My Lord.

Ham. Are you faire?

Ophe. What meanes your Lordship?

Ham. That if you be honest and faire, your Honesty
should admit no discourse to your Beautie.

Ophe. Could Beautie my Lord, haue better Comerce
then your Honestie?

Ham. I trulie : for the power of Beautie, will sooner
transforme Honestie from what it is, to a Bawd, then the
force of Honestie can translate Beautie into his likenesse.
This was sometime a Paradox, but now the time giues it
proofe. I did loue you once.

Ophe. Indeed my Lord, you made me beleeue so.

Ham. You should not haue beleeued me. For vertue
cannot so innocculate our old stocke, but we shall rellish
of it. I loued you not.

Ophe. I was the more deceiued.

Ham. Get thee to a Nunnerie. Why would'st thou
be a breeder of Sinners? I am my selfe indifferent honest,
but yet I could accuse me of such things, that it were better my Mother had not borne me. I am very prowd, re-
uengefull, Ambitious, with more offences at my becke,
then I haue thoughts to put them in imagination, to giue
them shape, or time to acte them in. What should such

Fel-

Fellowes as I do, crawling betweene Heauen and Earth.
We are arrant Knaues all, beleeue none of vs. Goe thy
wayes to a Nunnery. Where's your Father?

Ophe. At home, my Lord.

Ham. Let the doores be shut vpon him, that he may
play the Foole no way, but in's owne house. Farewell.

Ophe. O helpe him, you sweet Heauens.

Ham. If thou doest Marry, Ile giue thee this Plague
for thy Dowrie. Be thou as chast as Ice, as pure as Snow,
thou shalt not escape Calumny. Get thee to a Nunnery.
Go, Farewell. Or if thou wilt needs Marry, marry a fool:
for Wise men know well enough, what monsters you
make of them. To a Nunnery go, and quickly too. Far-
well.

Ophe. O heauenly Powers, restore him.

Ham. I haue heard of your pratlings too wel enough.
God has giuen you one pace, and you make your selfe another: you gidge, you amble, and you lispe, and nickname
Gods creatures, and make your Wantonnesse, your Ignorance. Go too, Ile no more on't, it hath made me mad.
I say, we will haue no more Marriages.   Those that are
married already, all but one shall liue, the rest shall keep
as they are. To a Nunnery, go.   *Exit Hamlet*

Ophe. O what a Noble minde is heere o're-throwne?
The Courtiers, Soldiers, Schollers: Eye, tongue, sword,
Th'expectansie and Rose of the faire State,
The glasse of Fashion, and the mould of Forme,
Th'obseru'd of all Obseruers, quite, quite downe.
Haue I of Ladies most deiect and wretched,
That suck'd the Honie of his Musicke Vowes:
Now see that Noble, and most Soueraigne Reason,
Like sweet Bels iangled out of tune, and harsh,
That vnmatch'd Forme and Feature of blowne youth,
Blasted with extasie. Oh woe is me,
T'haue seene what I haue seene: see what I see.

Enter King, and Polonius.

King. Loue? His affections do not that way tend,
Nor what he spake, though it lack'd Forme a little,
Was not like Madnesse. There's something in his soule?
O're which his Melancholly sits on brood,
And I do doubt the hatch, and the disclose
Will be some danger, which to preuent
I haue in quicke determination
Thus set it downe. He shall with speed to England
For the demand of our neglected Tribute:
Haply the Seas and Countries different
With variable Obiects, shall expell
This something setled matter in his heart:
Whereon his Braines still beating, puts him thus
From fashion of himselfe. What thinke you on't?

Pol. It shall do well. But yet do I beleeue
The Origin and Commencement of this greefe
Sprung from neglected loue. How now *Ophelia?*
You neede not tell vs, what Lord *Hamlet* saide,
We heard it all. My Lord, do as you please,
But if you hold it fit after the Play,
Let his Queene Mother all alone intreat him
To shew his Greefes: let her be round with him,
And Ile be plac'd so, please you in the eare
Of all their Conference. If she finde him not,
To England send him: Or confine him where
Your wisedome best shall thinke.

King. It shall be so:
Madnesse in great Ones, must not vnwatch'd go.
           Exeunt.

Enter Hamlet, and two or three of the Players.

Ham. Speake the Speech I pray you, as I pronounc'd
it to you trippingly on the Tongue: But if you mouth it,
as many of your Players do, I had as liue the Town-Cryer
had spoke my Lines: Nor do not saw the Ayre too much
your hand thus, but vse all gently; for in the verie Tor-
rent, Tempest, and (as I may say) the Whirle-winde of
Passion, you must acquire and beget a Temperance that
may giue it Smoothnesse. O it offends mee to the Soule,
to see a robustious Pery-wig-pated Fellow, teare a Passion to tatters, to verie ragges, to split the eares of the
Groundlings: who (for the most part) are capeable of
nothing, but inexplicable dumbe shewes, & noise: I could
haue such a Fellow whipt for o're-doing Termagant: it
out-*Herod's Herod.* Pray you auoid it.

Player. I warrant your Honor.

Ham. Be not too tame neyther: but let your owne
Discretion be your Tutor. Sute the Action to the Word,
the Word to the Action, with this speciall obseruance:
That you ore-stop not the modestie of Nature; for any
thing so ouer-done, is fro the purpose of Playing, whose
end both at the first and now, was and is, to hold as 'twer
the Mirrour vp to Nature; to shew Vertue her owne
Feature, Scorne her owne Image, and the verie Age and
Bodie of the Time, his forme and pressure. Now, this
ouer-done, or come tardie off, though it make the vnskil-
full laugh, cannot but make the Iudicious greeue; The
censure of the which One, must in your allowance o're-
way a whole Theater of Others. Oh, there bee Players
that I haue seene Play, and heard others praise, and that
highly (not to speake it prophanely) that neyther hauing
the accent of Christians, nor the gate of Christian, Pagan,
or Norman, haue so strutted and bellowed, that I haue
thought some of Natures Iourney-men had made men,
and not made them well, they imitated Humanity so ab-
hominably.

Play. I hope we haue reform'd that indifferently with
vs, Sir.

Ham. O reforme it altogether. And let those that
play your Clownes, speake no more then is set downe for
them. For there be of them, that will themselues laugh,
to set on some quantitie of barren Spectators to laugh
too, though in the meane time, some necessary Question
of the Play be then to be considered: that's Villanous, &
shewes a most pittifull Ambition in the Foole that vses
it. Go make you readie.   *Exit Players.*

Enter Polonius, Rosincrance, and Guildensterne.

How now my Lord,
Will the King heare this peece of Worke?

Pol. And the Queene too, and that presently.

Ham. Bid the Players make hast.   *Exit Polonius.*
Will you two helpe to hasten them?

Both. We will my Lord.   *Exeunt.*

Enter Horatio.

Ham. What hoa, *Horatio?*

Hora. Heere sweet Lord, at your Seruice.

Ham. Horatio, thou art eene as iust a man
As ere my Conuersation coap'd withall.

Hora. O my deere Lord.

Ham. Nay do not thinke I flatter:
For what aduancement may I hope from thee,
That no Reuennew hast, but thy good spirits

                                         To

To feed & cloath thee. Why shold the poor be flatter'd?
No, let the Candied tongue, like absurd pompe,
And crooke the pregnant Hindges of the knee,
Where thrift may follow faining? Dost thou heare,
Since my deere Soule was Mistris of my choyse,
And could of men distinguish, her election
Hath seal'd thee for her selfe. For thou hast bene
As one in suffering all, that suffers nothing.
A man that Fortunes buffets, and Rewards
Hath 'tane with equall Thankes. And blest are those,
Whose Blood and Iudgement are so well co-mingled,
That they are not a Pipe for Fortunes finger,
To sound what stop she please. Giue me that man,
That is not Passions Slaue, and I will weare him
In my hearts Core: I, in my Heart of heart,
As I do thee. Something too much of this.
There is a Play to night before the King,
One Scœne of it comes neere the Circumstance
Which I haue told thee, of my Fathers death.
I prythee, when thou see'st that Acte a-foot,
Euen with the verie Comment of my Soule
Obserue mine Vnkle: If his occulted guilt,
Do not it selfe vnkennell in one speech,
It is a damned Ghost that we haue seene:
And my Imaginations are as foule
As Vulcans Stythe. Giue him needfull note,
For I mine eyes will riuet to his Face:
And after we will both our iudgements ioyne,
To censure of his seeming.

Hora. Well my Lord.
If he steale ought the whil'st this Play is Playing,
And scape detecting, I will pay the Theft.

Enter King, Queene, Polonius, Ophelia, Rosincrance,
Guildensterne, and other Lords attendant with
his Guard carrying Torches. Danish
March. Sound a Flourish.

Ham. They are comming to the Play: I must be idle.
Get you a place.

King. How fares our Cosin *Hamlet?*

Ham. Excellent Ifaith, of the Camelions dish: I eate
the Ayre promise-cramm'd, you cannot feed Capons so.

King. I haue nothing with this answer *Hamlet,* these
words are not mine.

Ham. No, nor mine. Now my Lord, you plaid once
i'th'Vniuersity, you say?

Polon. That I did my Lord, and was accounted a good
Actor.

Ham. And what did you enact?

Pol. I did enact *Iulius Cæsar,* I was kill'd i'th'Capitol:
Brutus kill'd me.

Ham. It was a bruite part of him, to kill so Capitall a
Calfe there. Be the Players ready?

Rosin. I my Lord, they stay vpon your patience.

Qu. Come hither my good *Hamlet,* sit by me.

Ha. No good Mother, here's Mettle more attractiue.

Pol. Oh ho, do you marke that?

Ham. Ladie, shall I lye in your Lap?

Ophe. No my Lord.

Ham. I meane, my Head vpon your Lap?

Ophe. I my Lord.

Ham. Do you thinke I meant Country matters?

Ophe. I thinke nothing, my Lord.

Ham. That's a faire thought to ly between Maids legs

Ophe. What is my Lord?

Ham. Nothing.

Ophe. You are merrie, my Lord?

Ham. Who I?

Ophe. I my Lord.

Ham. Oh God, your onely Iigge-maker: what should
a man do, but be merrie. For looke you how cheerefully my Mother lookes, and my Father dyed within's two
Houres.

Ophe. Nay, 'tis twice two moneths, my Lord.

Ham. So long? Nay then let the Diuel weare blacke,
for Ile haue a suite of Sables. Oh Heauens! dye two moneths ago, and not forgotten yet? Then there's hope, a
great mans Memorie, may out-liue his life halfe a yeare:
But byrlady he must builde Churches then: or else shall
he suffer not thinking on, with the Hoby-horsse, whose
Epitaph is, For o, For o, the Hoby-horse is forgot.

Hoboyes play. The dumbe shew enters.
Enter a King and Queene, very louingly; the Queene embra-
cing him. She kneeles, and makes shew of Protestation vnto
him. He takes her vp, and declines his head vpon her neck.
Layes him downe vpon a Banke of Flowers. She seeing him
a-sleepe, leaues him. Anon comes in a Fellow, takes off his
Crowne, kisses it, and powres poyson in the Kings eares, and
Exits. The Queene returnes, findes the King dead, and
makes passionate Action. The Poysoner, with some two or
three Mutes comes in againe, seeming to lament with her.
The dead body is carried away: The Poysoner Wooes the
Queene with Gifts, she seemes loath and vnwilling awhile,
but in the end, accepts his loue. *Exeunt*

Ophe. What meanes this, my Lord?

Ham. Marry this is Miching *Malicho,* that meanes
Mischeefe.

Ophe. Belike this shew imports the Argument of the
Play?

Ham. We shall know by these Fellowes: the Players
cannot keepe counsell, they'l tell all.

Ophe. Will they tell vs what this shew meant?

Ham. I, or any shew that you'l shew him. Bee not
you asham'd to shew, hee'l not shame to tell you what it
meanes.

Ophe. You are naught, you are naught, Ile marke the
Play.

Enter Prologue.
For vs, and for our Tragedie,
Heere stooping to your Clemencie:
We begge your hearing Patientlie.

Ham. Is this a Prologue, or the Poesie of a Ring?

Ophe. 'Tis briefe my Lord.

Ham. As Womans loue.

Enter King and his Queene.
King. Full thirtie times hath Phœbus Cart gon round,
Neptunes salt Wash, and *Tellus* Orbed ground:
And thirtie dozen Moones with borrowed sheene,
About the World haue times twelue thirties beene,
Since loue our hearts, and *Hymen* did our hands
Vnite comutuall, in most sacred Bands.

Bap. So many iournies may the Sunne and Moone
Make vs againe count o're, ere loue be done.
But woe is me, you are so sicke of late,
So farre from cheere, and from your forme state,
That I distrust you: yet though I distrust,
Discomfort you (my Lord) it nothing must:
For womens Feare and Loue, holds quantitie,

In

In neither ought, or in extremity :
Now what my loue is, proofe hath made you know,
And as my Loue is siz'd, my Feare is so.

  King. Faith I must leaue thee Loue, and shortly too :
My operant Powers my Functions leaue to do :
And thou shalt liue in this faire world behinde,
Honour'd, belou'd, and haply, one as kinde.
For Husband shalt thou——

  Bap. Oh confound the rest :
Such Loue, must needs be Treason in my brest :
In second Husband, let me be accurst,
None wed the second, but who kill'd the first.

  Ham. Wormwood, Wormwood.

  Bapt. The instances that second Marriage moue,
Are base respects of Thrift, but none of Loue.
A second time, I kill my Husband dead,
When second Husband kisses me in Bed.

  King. I do beleeue you. Think what now you speak :
But what we do determine, oft we breake :
Purpose is but the slaue to Memorie,
Of violent Birth, but poore validitie :
Which now like Fruite vnripe stickes on the Tree,
But fall vnshaken, when they mellow bee.
Most necessary 'tis, that we forget
To pay our selues, what to our selues is debt :
What to our selues in passion we propose,
The passion ending, doth the purpose lose.
The violence of other Greefe or Ioy,
Their owne ennactors with themselues destroy :
Where Ioy most Reuels, Greefe doth most lament ;
Greefe ioyes, Ioy greeues on slender accident.
This world is not for aye, nor 'tis not strange
That euen our Loues should with our Fortunes change.
For 'tis a question left vs yet to proue,
Whether Loue lead Fortune, or else Fortune Loue.
The great man downe, you marke his fauourites flies,
The poore aduanc'd, makes Friends of Enemies :
And hitherto doth Loue on Fortune tend,
For who not needs, shall neuer lacke a Frend :
And who in want a hollow Friend doth try,
Directly seasons him his Enemie.
But orderly to end, where I begun,
Our Willes and Fates do so contrary run,
That our Deuices still are ouerthrowne,
Our thoughts are ours, their ends none of our owne.
So thinke thou wilt no second Husband wed.
But die thy thoughts, when thy first Lord is dead.

  Bap. Nor Earth to giue me food, nor Heauen light,
Sport and repose locke from me day and night :
Each opposite that blankes the face of ioy,
Meet what I would haue well, and it destroy :
Both heere, and hence, pursue me lasting strife,
If once a Widdow, euer I be Wife.

  Ham. If she should breake it now.

  King. 'Tis deepely sworne :
Sweet, leaue me heere a while,
My spirits grow dull, and faine I would beguile
The tedious day with sleepe.

  Qu. Sleepe rocke thy Braine,   *Sleepes*
And neuer come mischance betweene vs twaine. *Exit*

  Ham. Madam, how like you this Play?

  Qu. The Lady protests to much me thinkes.

  Ham. Oh but shee'l keepe her word.

  King. Haue you heard the Argument, is there no Offence in't ?

  Ham. No, no, they do but iest, poyson in iest, no Of-

fence i'th'world.

  King. What do you call the Play ?

  Ham. The Mouse-trap : Marry how ? Tropically :
This Play is the Image of a murder done in *Vienna: Gon-*
zago is the Dukes name, his wife *Baptista* : you shall see
anon : 'tis a knauish peece of worke : But what o'that ?
Your Maiestie, and wee that haue free soules, it touches
vs not : let the gall'd iade winch : our withers are vnrung.

      Enter Lucianus.

This is one *Lucianus* nephew to the King.

  Ophe. You are a good Chorus, my Lord.

  Ham. I could interpret betweene you and your loue :
if I could see the Puppets dallying.

  Ophe. You are keene my Lord, you are keene.

  Ham. It would cost you a groaning, to take off my
edge.

  Ophe. Still better and worse.

  Ham. So you mistake Husbands.
Begin Murderer. Pox, leaue thy damnable Faces, and
begin. Come, the croaking Rauen doth bellow for Reuenge.

  Lucian. Thoughts blacke, hands apt,
Drugges fit, and Time agreeing :
Confederate season, else, no Creature seeing :
Thou mixture ranke, of Midnight Weeds collected,
With Hecats Ban, thrice blasted, thrice infected,
Thy naturall Magicke, and dire propertie,
On wholsome life, vsurpe immediately.

      Powres the poyson in his eares.

  Ham. He poysons him i'th Garden for's estate : His
name's *Gonzago* : the Story is extant and writ in choyce
Italian. You shall see anon how the Murtherer gets the
loue of *Gonzago's* wife.

  Ophe. The King rises.

  Ham. What, frighted with false fire.

  Qu. How fares my Lord?

  Pol. Giue o're the Play.

  King. Giue me some Light. Away.

  All. Lights, Lights, Lights.   *Exeunt*

      Manet Hamlet & Horatio.

  Ham. Why let the strucken Deere go weepe,
The Hart vngalled play :
For some must watch, while some must sleepe ;
So runnes the world away.
Would not this Sir, and a Forrest of Feathers, if the rest of
my Fortunes turne Turke with me ; with two Prouinciall
Roses on my rac'd Shooes, get me a Fellowship in a crie
of Players sir.

  Hor. Halfe a share.

  Ham. A whole one I,
For thou dost know : Oh *Damon* deere,
This Realme dismantled was of Ioue himselfe,
And now reignes heere.
A verie verie Paiocke.

  Hora. You might haue Rim'd.

  Ham. Oh good *Horatio*, Ile take the Ghosts word for
a thousand pound. Did'st perceiue ?

  Hora. Verie well my Lord.

  Ham. Vpon the talke of the poysoning?

  Hora. I did verie well note him.

     Enter Rosincrance and Guildensterne.

  Ham. Oh, ha? Come some Musick. Come ÿ Recorders:
For if the King like not the Comedie,
Why then belike he likes it not perdie.
Come some Musicke.

  Guild. Good my Lord, vouchsafe me a word with you.

                   Ham.

Ham. Sir, a whole Hiſtory.

Guild. The King, ſir.

Ham. I ſir, what of him?

Guild. Is in his retyrement, maruellous diſtemper'd.

Ham. With drinke Sir?

Guild. No my Lord, rather with choller.

Ham. Your wiſedome ſhould ſhew it ſelfe more richer, to ſignifie this to his Doctor: for for me to put him
to his Purgation, would perhaps plundge him into farre
more Choller.

Guild. Good my Lord put your diſcourſe into ſome
frame, and ſtart not ſo wildely from my affayre.

Ham. I am tame Sir, pronounce.

Guild. The Queene your Mother, in moſt great affliction of ſpirit, hath ſent me to you.

Ham. You are welcome.

Guild. Nay, good my Lord, this courteſie is not of
the right breed. If it ſhall pleaſe you to make me a wholſome anſwer, I will doe your Mothers command'ment:
if not, your pardon, and my returne ſhall bee the end of
my Buſineſſe.

Ham. Sir, I cannot.

Guild. What, my Lord?

Ham. Make you a wholſome anſwere: my wits diſ-
eas'd. But ſir, ſuch anſwers as I can make, you ſhal command: or rather you ſay, my Mother: therfore no more
but to the matter. My Mother you ſay.

Roſin. Then thus ſhe ſayes: your behauior hath ſtroke
her into amazement, and admiration.

Ham. Oh wonderfull Sonne, that can ſo aſtoniſh a
Mother. But is there no ſequell at the heeles of this Mothers admiration?

Roſin. She deſires to ſpeake with you in her Cloſſet,
ere you go to bed.

Ham. We ſhall obey, were ſhe ten times our Mother.
Haue you any further Trade with vs?

Roſin. My Lord, you once did loue me.

Ham. So I do ſtill, by theſe pickers and ſtealers.

Roſin. Good my Lord, what is your cauſe of diſtemper? You do freely barre the doore of your owne Liber-
tie, if you deny your greefes to your Friend.

Ham. Sir I lacke Aduancement.

Roſin. How can that be, when you haue the voyce of
the King himſelfe, for your Succeſſion in Denmarke?

Ham. I, but while the graſſe growes, the Prouerbe is
ſomething muſty.

Enter one with a Recorder.

O the Recorder. Let me ſee, to withdraw with you, why
do you go about to recouer the winde of mee, as if you
would driue me into a toyle?

Guild. O my Lord, if my Dutie be too bold, my loue
is too vnmannerly.

Ham. I do not well vnderſtand that. Will you play
vpon this Pipe?

Guild. My Lord, I cannot.

Ham. I pray you.

Guild. Beleeue me, I cannot.

Ham. I do beſeech you.

Guild. I know no touch of it, my Lord.

Ham. 'Tis as eaſie as lying: gouerne theſe Ventiges
with your finger and thumbe, giue it breath with your
mouth, and it will diſcourſe moſt excellent Muſicke.
Looke you, theſe are the ſtoppes.

Guild. But theſe cannot I command to any vtterance
of hermony, I haue not the skill.

Ham. Why looke you now, how vnworthy a thing
you make of me: you would play vpon mee; you would
ſeeme to know my ſtops: you would pluck out the heart
of my Myſterie; you would ſound mee from my loweſt
Note, to the top of my Compaſſe: and there is much Muſicke, excellent Voice, in this little Organe, yet cannot
you make it. Why do you thinke, that I am eaſier to bee
plaid on, then a Pipe? Call me what Inſtrument you will,
though you can fret me, you cannot play vpon me. God
bleſſe you Sir.

Enter Polonius.

Polon. My Lord; the Queene would ſpeak with you,
and preſently.

Ham. Do you ſee that Clowd? that's almoſt in ſhape
like a Camell.

Polon. By'th'Miſſe, and it's like a Camell indeed.

Ham. Me thinkes it is like a Weazell.

Polon. It is back'd like a Weazell.

Ham. Or like a Whale?

Polon. Verie like a Whale.

Ham. Then will I come to my Mother, by and by:
They foole me to the top of my bent.
I will come by and by.

Polon. I will ſay ſo.   *Exit.*

Ham. By and by, is eaſily ſaid. Leaue me Friends:
'Tis now the verie witching time of night,
When Churchyards yawne, and Hell it ſelfe breaths out
Contagion to this world. Now could I drink hot blood,
And do ſuch bitter buſineſſe as the day
Would quake to looke on. Soft now, to my Mother:
Oh Heart, looſe not thy Nature; let not euer
The Soule of *Nero*, enter this firme boſome:
Let me be cruell, not vnnaturall,
I will ſpeake Daggers to her, but vſe none:
My Tongue and Soule in this be Hypocrites.
How in my words ſomeuer ſhe be ſhent,
To giue them Seales, neuer my Soule conſent.

Enter King, Roſincrance, and Guilderſterne.

King. I like him not, nor ſtands it ſafe with vs,
To let his madneſſe range. Therefore prepare you,
I your Commiſſion will forthwith diſpatch,
And he to England ſhall along with you:
The termes of our eſtate, may not endure
Hazard ſo dangerous as doth hourely grow
Out of his Lunacies.

Guild. We will our ſelues prouide:
Moſt holie and Religious feare it is
To keepe thoſe many many bodies ſafe
That liue and feede vpon your Maieſtie.

Roſin. The ſingle
And peculiar life is bound
With all the ſtrength and Armour of the minde,
To keepe it ſelfe from noyance: but much more,
That Spirit, vpon whoſe ſpirit depends and reſts
The liues of many, the ceaſe of Maieſtie
Dies not alone; but like a Gulfe doth draw
What's neere it, with it. It is a maſſie wheele
Fixt on the Sommet of the higheſt Mount,
To whoſe huge Spoakes, ten thouſand leſſer things
Are mortiz'd and adioyn'd: which when it falles,
Each ſmall annexment, pettie conſequence
Attends the boyſtrous Ruine. Neuer alone
Did the King ſighe, but with a generall grone.

King. Arme you, I pray you to this ſpeedie Voyage;
For we will Fetters put vpon this feare,

Which now goes too free-footed.

Both. We will haste vs.   *Exeunt Gent.*

Enter Polonius.

Pol. My Lord, he's going to his Mothers Closset:
Behinde the Arras Ile conuey my selfe
To heare the Procesfe. Ile warrant shee'l tax him home,
And as you said, and wisely was it said,
'Tis meete that some more audience then a Mother,
Since Nature makes them partiall, should o're-heare
The speech of vantage. Fare you well my Liege,
Ile call vpon you ere you go to bed,
And tell you what I know.

King. Thankes deere my Lord.
Oh my offence is ranke, it smels to heauen,
It hath the primall eldest curse vpon't,
A Brothers murther. Pray can I not,
Though inclination be as sharpe as will:
My stronger guilt, defeats my strong intent,
And like a man to double businesse bound,
I stand in pause where I shall first begin,
And both neglect; what if this cursed hand
Were thicker then it selfe with Brothers blood,
Is there not Raine enough in the sweet Heauens
To wash it white as Snow? Whereto serues mercy,
But to confront the visage of Offence?
And what's in Prayer, but this two-fold force,
To be fore-stalled ere we come to fall,
Or pardon'd being downe? Then Ile looke vp,
My fault is past. But oh, what forme of Prayer
Can serue my turne? Forgiue me my foule Murther:
That cannot be, since I am still possest
Of those effects for which I did the Murther.
My Crowne, mine owne Ambition, and my Queene:
May one be pardon'd, and retaine th'offence?
In the corrupted currants of this world,
Offences gilded hand may shoue by Iustice,
And oft 'tis seene, the wicked prize it selfe
Buyes out the Law; but 'tis not so aboue,
There is no shuffling, there the Action lyes
In his true Nature, and we our selues compell'd
Euen to the teeth and forehead of our faults,
To giue in euidence. What then? What rests?
Try what Repentance can. What can it not?
Yet what can it, when one cannot repent?
Oh wretched state! Oh bosome, blacke as death!
Oh limed soule, that strugling to be free,
Art more ingag'd: Helpe Angels, make assay:
Bow stubborne knees, and heart with strings of Steele,
Be soft as sinewes of the new-borne Babe,
All may be well.

Enter Hamlet.

Ham. Now might I do it pat, now he is praying,
And now Ile doo't, and so he goes to Heauen,
And so am I reueng'd: that would be scann'd,
A Villaine killes my Father, and for that
I his foule Sonne, do this same Villaine send
To heauen. Oh this is hyre and Sallery, not Reuenge.
He tooke my Father grossely, full of bread,
With all his Crimes broad blowne, as fresh as May,
And how his Audit stands, who knowes, saue Heauen:
But in our circumstance and course of thought
'Tis heauie with him: and am I then reueng'd,
To take him in the purging of his Soule,
When he is fit and season'd for his passage? No.
Vp Sword, and know thou a more horrid hent

When he is drunke asleepe: or in his Rage,
Or in th'incestuous pleasure of his bed,
At gaming, swearing, or about some acte
That ha's no rellish of Saluation in't,
Then trip him, that his heeles may kicke at Heauen,
And that his Soule may be as damn'd aud blacke
As Hell, whereto it goes. My Mother stayes,
This Physicke but prolongs thy sickly dayes. *Exit.*

King. My words flye vp, my thoughts remain below,
Words without thoughts, neuer to Heauen go. *Exit.*

Enter Queene and Polonius.

Pol. He will come straight:
Looke you lay home to him,
Tell him his prankes haue been too broad to beare with,
And that your Grace hath scree'nd, and stoode betweene
Much heate, and him. Ile silence me e'ene heere:
Pray you be round with him.

Ham. within. Mother, mother, mother.

Qu. Ile warrant you, feare me not.
Withdraw, I heare him comming.

Enter Hamlet.

Ham. Now Mother, what's the matter?

Qu. Hamlet, thou hast thy Father much offended.

Ham. Mother, you haue my Father much offended.

Qu. Come, come, you answer with an idle tongue.

Ham. Go, go, you question with an idle tongue.

Qu. Why how now *Hamlet?*

Ham. Whats the matter now?

Qu. Haue you forgot me?

Ham. No by the Rood, not so:
You are the Queene, your Husbands Brothers wife,
But would you were not so. You are my Mother.

Qu. Nay, then Ile set those to you that can speake.

Ham. Come, come, and sit you downe, you shall not
boudge:
You go not till I set you vp a glasse,
Where you may see the inmost part of you?

Qu. What wilt thou do? thou wilt not murther me?
Helpe, helpe, hoa.

Pol. What hoa, helpe, helpe, helpe.

Ham. How now, a Rat? dead for a Ducate, dead.

Pol. Oh I am slaine.   *Killes Polonius.*

Qu. Oh me, what hast thou done?

Ham. Nay I know not, is it the King?

Qu. Oh what a rash, and bloody deed is this?

Ham. A bloody deed, almost as bad good Mother,
As kill a King, and marrie with his Brother.

Qu. As kill a King?

Ham. I Lady, 'twas my word.
Thou wretched, rash, intruding foole farewell,
I tooke thee for thy Betters, take thy Fortune,
Thou find'st to be too busie, is some danger.
Leaue wringing of your hands, peace, sit you downe,
And let me wring your heart, for so I shall
If it be made of penetrable stuffe;
If damned Custome haue not braz'd it so,
That it is proofe and bulwarke against Sense.

Qu. What haue I done, that thou dar'st wag thy tong,
In noise so rude against me?

Ham. Such an Act
That blurres the grace and blush of Modestie,
Cals Vertue Hypocrite, takes off the Rose
From the faire forehead of an innocent loue,
And makes a blister there. Makes marriage vowes
As false as Dicers Oathes. Oh such a deed,

As

As from the body of Contraction pluckes
The very soule, and sweete Religion makes
A rapsodie of words. Heauens face doth glow,
Yea this solidity and compound masse,
With triftfull visage as againt the doome,
Is thought-sicke at the act.

Qu. Aye me; what act, that roares so lowd, & thunders in the Index.

Ham. Looke heere vpon this Picture, and on this,
The counterfet presentment of two Brothers:
See what a grace was seated on his Brow,
Hyperions curles, the front of Ioue himselfe,
An eye like Mars, to threaten or command
A Station, like the Herald Mercurie
New lighted on a heauen kissing hill:
A Combination, and a forme indeed,
Where euery God did seeme to set his Seale,
To giue the world assurance of a man.
This was your Husband. Looke you now what followes.
Heere is your Husband, like a Mildew'd eare
Blasting his wholsom breath. Haue you eyes?
Could you on this faire Mountaine leaue to feed,
And batten on this Moore? Ha? Haue you eyes?
You cannot call it Loue: For at your age,
The hey-day in the blood is tame, it's humble,
And waites vpon the Iudgement: and what Iudgement
Would step from this, to this? What diuell was't,
That thus hath cousend you at hoodman-blinde?
O Shame! where is thy Blush? Rebellious Hell,
If thou canst mutine in a Matrons bones,
To flaming youth, let Vertue be as waxe,
And melt in her owne fire. Proclaime no shame,
When the compulsiue Ardure giues the charge,
Since Frost it selfe, as actiuely doth burne,
As Reason panders Will.

Qu. O *Hamlet*, speake no more.
Thou turn'st mine eyes into my very soule,
And there I see such blacke and grained spots,
As will not leaue their Tinct.

Ham. Nay, but to liue
In the ranke sweat of an enseamed bed,
Stew'd in Corruption; honying and making loue
Ouer the nasty Stye.

Qu. Oh speake to me, no more,
These words like Daggers enter in mine eares.
No more sweet *Hamlet*.

Ham. A Murderer, and a Villaine:
A Slaue, that is not twentieth part the tythe
Of your precedent Lord. A vice of Kings,
A Cutpurse of the Empire and the Rule.
That from a shelfe, the precious Diadem stole,
And put it in his Pocket.

Qu. No more.

Enter Ghost.

Ham. A King of shreds and patches.
Saue me; and houer o're me with your wings
You heauenly Guards. What would you gracious figure?

Qu. Alas he's mad.

Ham. Do you not come your tardy Sonne to chide,
That laps't in Time and Passion, lets go by
Th'important acting of your dread command? Oh say.

Ghost. Do not forget: this Visitation
Is but to whet thy almost blunted purpose.
But looke, Amazement on thy Mother sits;
O step betweene her, and her fighting Soule,
Conceit in weakest bodies, strongest workes.

Speake to her *Hamlet*.

Ham. How is it with you Lady?

Qu. Alas, how is't with you?
That you bend your eye on vacancie,
And with their corporall ayre do hold discourse.
Forth at your eyes, your spirits wildely peepe,
And as the sleeping Soldiours in th'Alarme,
Your bedded haire, like life in excrements,
Start vp, and stand an end. Oh gentle Sonne,
Vpon the heate and flame of thy distemp'er
Sprinkle coole patience. Whereon do you looke?

Ham. On him, on him: look you how pale he glares,
His forme and cause conioyn'd, preaching to stones,
Would make them capeable. Do not looke vpon me,
Least with this pitteous action you conuert
My sterne effects: then what I haue to do,
Will want true colour; teares perchance for blood.

Qu. To who do you speake this?

Ham. Do you see nothing there?

Qu. Nothing at all, yet all that is I see.

Ham. Nor did you nothing heare?

Qu. No, nothing but our selues.

Ham. Why look you there: looke how it steals away:
My Father in his habite, as he liued,
Looke where he goes euen now out at the Portall. *Exit.*

Qu. This is the very coynage of your Braine,
This bodilesse Creation extasie is very cunning in.

Ham. Extasie?
My Pulse as yours doth temperately keepe time,
And makes as healthfull Musicke. It is not madnesse
That I haue vttered; bring me to the Test
And I the matter will re-word: which madnesse
Would gamboll from. Mother, for loue of Grace,
Lay not a flattering Vnction to your soule,
That not your trespasse, but my madnesse speakes:
It will but skin and filme the Vlcerous place,
Whil'st ranke Corruption mining all within,
Infects vnseene. Confesse your selfe to Heauen,
Repent what's past, auoyd what is to come,
And do not spred the Compost or the Weedes,
To make them ranke. Forgiue me this my Vertue,
For in the fatnesse of this pursie times,
Vertue it selfe, of Vice must pardon begge,
Yea courb, and woe, for leaue to do him good.

Qu. Oh *Hamlet*,
Thou hast cleft my heart in twaine.

Ham. O throw away the worser part of it,
And liue the purer with the other halfe.
Good night, but go not to mine Vnkles bed,
Assume a Vertue, if you haue it not, refraine to night;
And that shall lend a kinde of easinesse
To the next abstinence. Once more goodnight,
And when you are desirous to be blest,
Ile blessing begge of you. For this same Lord,
I do repent: but heauen hath pleas'd it so,
To punish me with this, and this with me,
That I must be their Scourge and Minister.
I will bestow him, and will answer well
The death I gaue him: so againe, good night.
I must be cruell, onely to be kinde;
Thus bad begins, and worse remaines behinde.

Qu. What shall I do?

Ham. Not this by no meanes that I bid you do:
Let the blunt King tempt you againe to bed,
Pinch Wanton on your cheeke, call you his Mouse,
And let him for a paire of reechie kisses,

Or padling in your necke with his damn'd Fingers,
Make you to rauell all this matter out,
That I essentially am not in madnesse,
But made in craft. 'Twere good you let him know,
For who that's but a Queene, faire, sober, wise,
Would from a Paddocke, from a Bat, a Gibbe,
Such deere concernings hide, Who would do so,
No in despight of Sense and Secrecie,
Vnpegge the Basket on the houses top:
Let the Birds flye, and like the famous Ape
To try Conclusions in the Basket, creepe
And breake your owne necke downe.

Qu. Be thou assur'd, if words be made of breath,
And breath of life: I haue no life to breath
What thou hast saide to me.

Ham. I must to England, you know that?

Qu. Alacke I had forgot: 'Tis so concluded on.

Ham. This man shall set me packing:
Ile lugge the Guts into the Neighbor roome,
Mother goodnight. Indeede this Counsellor
Is now most still, most secret, and most graue,
Who was in life, a foolish prating Knaue.
Come sir, to draw toward an end with you.
Good night Mother.

Exit Hamlet tugging in Polonius.
Enter King.

King. There's matters in these sighes.
These profound heaues
You must translate: Tis fit we vnderstand them.
Where is your Sonne?

Qu. Ah my good Lord, what haue I seene to night?

King. What *Gertrude?* How do's *Hamlet?*

Qu. Mad as the Seas, and winde, when both contend
Which is the Mightier, in his lawlesse fit
Behinde the Arras, hearing something stirre,
He whips his Rapier out, and cries a Rat, a Rat,
And in his brainish apprehension killes
The vnseene good old man.

King. Oh heauy deed:
It had bin so with vs had we beene there:
His Liberty is full of threats to all,
To you your selfe, to vs, to euery one.
Alas, how shall this bloody deede be answered?
It will be laide to vs, whose prouidence
Should haue kept short, restrain'd, and out of haunt,
This mad yong man. But so much was our loue,
We would not vnderstand what was most fit,
But like the Owner of a foule disease,
To keepe it from divulging, let's it feede
Euen on the pith of life. Where is he gone?

Qu. To draw apart the body he hath kild,
O're whom his very madnesse like some Oare
Among a Minerall of Mettels base
Shewes it selfe pure. He weepes for what is done.

King. Oh *Gertrude,* come away:
The Sun no sooner shall the Mountaines touch,
But we will ship him hence, and this vilde deed,
We must with all our Maiesty and Skill
Both countenance, and excuse. *Enter Rof. & Guild.*
Ho *Guildenstern:*
Friends both go ioyne you with some further ayde:
Hamlet in madnesse hath *Polonius* slaine,
And from his Mother Closset hath he drag'd him.
Go seeke him out, speake faire, and bring the body
Into the Chappell. I pray you hast in this. *Exit Gent.*
Come *Gertrude,* wee'l call vp our wisest friends,

To let them know both what we meane to do,
And what's vntimely done. Oh come away,
My soule is full of discord and dismay. *Exeunt.*

Enter Hamlet.

Ham. Safely stowed.

Gentlemen within. *Hamlet,* Lord *Hamlet.*

Ham. What noise? Who cals on *Hamlet?*
Oh heere they come. *Enter Rof. and Guildensterne.*

Ro. What haue you done my Lord with the dead body?

Ham. Compounded it with dust, whereto 'tis Kinne.

Rosin. Tell vs where 'tis, that we may take it thence,
And beare it to the Chappell.

Ham. Do not beleeue it.

Rosin. Beleeue what?

Ham. That I can keepe your counsell, and not mine
owne. Besides, to be demanded of a Spundge, what re-
plication should be made by the Sonne of a King.

Rosin. Take you me for a Spundge, my Lord?

Ham. I sir, that sokes vp the Kings Countenance, his
Rewards, his Authorities (but such Officers do the King
best seruice in the end. He keepes them like an Ape in
the corner of his iaw, first mouth'd to be last swallowed,
when he needes what you haue glean'd, it is but squee-
zing you, and Spundge you shall be dry againe.

Rosin. I vnderstand you not my Lord.

Ham. I am glad of it: a knauish speech sleepes in a
foolish eare.

Rosin. My Lord, you must tell vs where the body is,
and go with vs to the King.

Ham. The body is with the King, but the King is not
with the body. The King, is a thing ———

Guild. A thing my Lord?

Ham. Of nothing: bring me to him, hide Fox, and all
after. *Exeunt*

Enter King.

King. I haue sent to seeke him, and to find the bodie:
How dangerous is it that this man goes loose:
Yet must not we put the strong Law on him:
Hee's loued of the distracted multitude,
Who like not in their iudgement, but their eyes:
And where 'tis so, th'Offenders scourge is weigh'd
But neerer the offence: to beare all smooth, and euen,
This sodaine sending him away, must seeme
Deliberate pause, diseases desperate growne,
By desperate appliance are releeued,
Or not at all. *Enter Rosincrane.*
How now? What hath befalne?

Rosin. Where the dead body is bestow'd my Lord,
We cannot get from him.

King. But where is he?

Rosin. Without my Lord, guarded to know your
pleasure.

King. Bring him before vs.

Rosin. Hoa, *Guildensterne?* Bring in my Lord.

Enter Hamlet and Guildensterne.

King. Now *Hamlet,* where's *Polonius?*

Ham. At Supper.

King. At Supper? Where?

Ham. Not where he eats, but where he is eaten, a certaine conuocation of wormes are e'ne at him. Your worm
is your onely Emperor for diet. We fat all creatures else
to fat vs, and we fat our selfe for Magots. Your fat King,
and your leane Begger is but variable seruice to dishes,
but to one Table that's the end.

King. What dost thou meane by this?

Ham.

Ham. Nothing but to shew you how a King may go a Progresse through the guts of a Begger.

King. Where is *Polonius*.

Ham. In heauen, send thither to see. If your Messenger finde him not there, seeke him i'th other place your selfe : but indeed, if you finde him not this moneth, you shall nose him as you go vp the staires into the Lobby.

King. Go seeke him there.

Ham. He will stay till ye come.

K. *Hamlet*, this deed of thine, for thine especial safety Which we do tender, as we deerely greeue For that which thou hast done, must send thee hence With fierie Quicknesse. Therefore prepare thy selfe, The Barke is readie, and the winde at helpe, Th'Associates tend, and euery thing at bent For England.

Ham. For England ?

King. I *Hamlet*.

Ham. Good.

King. So is it, if thou knew'st our purposes.

Ham. I see a Cherube that see's him : but come, for England. Farewell deere Mother.

King. Thy louing Father *Hamlet*.

Hamlet. My Mother : Father and Mother is man and wife : man & wife is one flesh, and so my mother. Come, for England. *Exit*

King. Follow him at foote, Tempt him with speed aboord : Delay it not, Ile haue him hence to night. Away, for euery thing is Seal'd and done That else leanes on th'Affaire pray you make hast. And England, if my loue thou holdst at ought, As my great power thereof may giue thee sense, Since yet thy Cicatrice lookes raw and red After the Danish Sword, and thy free awe Payes homage to vs ; thou maist not coldly set Our Soueraigne Processe, which imports at full By Letters coniuring to that effect The present death of *Hamlet*. Do it England, For like the Hecticke in my blood he rages, And thou must cure me : Till I know 'tis done, How ere my happes, my ioyes were ne're begun. *Exit*

Enter Fortinbras with an Armie.

For. Go Captaine, from me greet the Danish King, Tell him that by his license, *Fortinbras* Claimes the conueyance of a promis'd March Ouer his Kingdome. You know the Rendeuous : If that his Maiesty would ought with vs, We shall expresse our dutie in his eye, And let him know so.

Cap. I will doo't, my Lord.

For. Go safely on. *Exit.*

Enter Queene and Horatio.

Qu. I will not speake with her.

Hor. She is importunate, indeed distract, her moode will needs be pittied.

Qu. What would she haue ?

Hor. She speakes much of her Father ; saies she heares There's trickes i'th'world, and hems, and beats her heart, Spurnes enuiously at Strawes, speakes things in doubt, That carry but halfe sense : Her speech is nothing, Yet the vnshaped vse of it doth moue The hearers to Collection ; they ayme at it, And botch the words vp fit to their owne thoughts, Which as her winkes, and nods, and gestures yeeld them,

Indeed would make one thinke there would be thought, Though nothing sure, yet much vnhappily.

Qu. 'Twere good she were spoken with, For she may strew dangerous coniectures In ill breeding minds. Let her come in. To my sicke soule (as sinnes true Nature is) Each toy seemes Prologue, to some great amisse, So full of Artlesse iealousie is guilt, It spill's it selfe, in fearing to be spilt.

Enter Ophelia distracted.

Ophe. Where is the beauteous Maiesty of Denmark.

Qu. How now *Ophelia*?

Ophe. How should I your true loue know from another one? By his Cockle hat and staffe, and his Sandal shoone.

Qu. Alas sweet Lady : what imports this Song?

Ophe. Say you? Nay pray you marke. He is dead and gone Lady, he is dead and gone, At his head a grasse-greene Turfe, at his heeles a stone.

Enter King.

Qu. Nay but *Ophelia*.

Ophe. Pray you marke. White his Shrow'd as the Mountaine Snow.

Qu. Alas looke heere my Lord.

Ophe. Larded with sweet flowers : Which bewept to the graue did not go, With true-loue showres.

King. How do ye, pretty Lady ?

Ophe. Well, God dil'd you. They say the Owle was a Bakers daughter. Lord, wee know what we are, but know not what we may be. God be at your Table.

King. Conceit vpon her Father.

Ophe. Pray you let's haue no words of this : but when they aske you what it meanes, say you this : To morrow is S. Valentines day, all in the morning betime, And I a Maid at your Window to be your Valentine. Then vp he rose, & don'd his clothes, & dupt the chamber dore, Let in the Maid, that out a Maid, neuer departed more.

King. Pretty *Ophelia*.

Ophe. Indeed la? without an oath Ile make an end ont. By gis, and by S. Charity, Alacke, and fie for shame : Yong men wil doo't, if they come too't, By Cocke they are too blame. Quoth she before you tumbled me, You promis'd me to Wed : So would I ha done by yonder Sunne, And thou hadst not come to my bed.

King. How long hath she bin this?

Ophe. I hope all will be well. We must bee patient, but I cannot choose but weepe, to thinke they should lay him i'th'cold ground : My brother shall knowe of it, and so I thanke you for your good counsell. Come, my Coach : Goodnight Ladies : Goodnight sweet Ladies : Goodnight, goodnight. *Exit.*

King. Follow her close, Giue her good watch I pray you : Oh this is the poyson of deepe greefe, it springs All from her Fathers death. Oh *Gertrude*, *Gertrude*, When sorrowes comes, they come not single spies, But in Battaliaes. First, her Father slaine, Next your Sonne gone, and he most violent Author Of his owne iust remoue : the people muddied, Thicke and vnwholsome in their thoughts, and whispers For good *Polonius* death ; and we haue done but greenly In hugger mugger to interre him. Poore *Ophelia* Diuided from her selfe, and her faire Iudgement.

Without the which we are Pictures, or meere Beasts.
Last, and as much containing as all these,
Her Brother is in secret come from France,
Keepes on his wonder, keepes himselfe in clouds,
And wants not Buzzers to infect his eare
With pestilent Speeches of his Fathers death,
Where in necessitie of matter Beggard,
Will nothing sticke our persons to Arraigne
In eare and eare. O my deere *Gertrude*, this,
Like to a murdering Peece in many places,
Giues me superfluous death.   *A Noise within.*

Enter a Messenger.

Qu. Alacke, what noyse is this?

King. Where are my *Switzers* ?
Let them guard the doore. What is the matter ?

Mes. Saue your selfe, my Lord.
The Ocean (ouer-peering of his List)
Eates not the Flats with more impittious haste
Then young *Laertes*, in a Riotous head,
Ore-beares your Officers, the rabble call him Lord,
And as the world were now but to begin,
Antiquity forgot, Custome not knowne,
The Ratifiers and props of euery word,
They cry choose we ? *Laertes* shall be King,
Caps, hands, and tongues, applaud it to the clouds,
Laertes shall be King, *Laertes* King.

Qu. How cheerefully on the false Traile they cry,
Oh this is Counter you false Danish Dogges.

Noise within.   *Enter Laertes.*

King. The doores are broke.

Laer. Where is the King, sirs ? Stand you all without.

All. No, let's come in.

Laer. I pray you giue me leaue.

Al. We will, we will.

Laer. I thanke you : Keepe the doore.
Oh thou vilde King, giue me my Father.

Qu. Calmely good *Laertes*.

Laer. That drop of blood, that calmes
Proclaimes me Bastard :
Cries Cuckold to my Father, brands the Harlot
Euen heere betweene the chaste vnsmirched brow
Of my true Mother.

King. What is the cause *Laertes*,
That thy Rebellion lookes so Gyant-like?
Let him go *Gertrude* : Do not feare our person :
There's such Diuinity doth hedge a King,
That Treason can but peepe to what it would,
Acts little of his will. Tell me *Laertes*,
Why thou art thus Incenst? Let him go *Gertrude*.
Speake man.

Laer. Where's my Father ?

King. Dead.

Qu. But not by him.

King. Let him demand his fill.

Laer. How came he dead ? Ile not be Iuggel'd with.
To hell Allegeance : Vowes, to the blackest diuell.
Conscience and Grace, to the profoundest Pit.
I dare Damnation : to this point I stand,
That both the worlds I giue to negligence,
Let come what comes : onely Ile be reueng'd
Most throughly for my Father.

King. Who shall stay you?

Laer. My Will, not all the world,
And for my meanes, Ile husband them so well,
They shall go farre with little.

King. Good *Laertes* :
If you desire to know the certaintie
Of your deere Fathers death, if writ in your reuenge,
That Soop-stake you will draw both Friend and Foe,
Winner and Looser.

Laer. None but his Enemies.

King. Will you know them then,

La. To his good Friends, thus wide Ile ope'my Armes :
And like the kinde Life-rend'ring Politician,
Repast them with my blood.

King. Why now you speake
Like a good Childe, and a true Gentleman.
That I am guiltlesse of your Fathers death,
And am most sensible in greefe for it,
It shall as leuell to your Iudgement pierce
As day do's to your eye.

A noise within. Let her come in.

Enter Ophelia.

Laer. How now? what noise is that?
Oh heate drie vp my Braines, teares seuen times salt,
Burne out the Sence and Vertue of mine eye.
By Heauen, thy madnesse shall be payed by waight,
Till our Scale turnes the beame. Oh Rose of May,
Deere Maid, kinde Sister, sweet *Ophelia* :
Oh Heauens, is't possible, a yong Maids wits,
Should be as mortall as an old mans life?
Nature is fine in Loue, and where 'tis fine,
It sends some precious instance of it selfe
After the thing it loues.

Ophe. They bore him bare fac'd on the Beer,
Hey non nony, nony, hey nony :
And on his graue raines many a teare,
Fare you well my Doue.

Laer. Had'st thou thy wits, and did'st perswade Reuenge, it could not moue thus.

Ophe. You must sing downe a-downe, and you call
him a-downe-a. Oh, how the wheele becomes it ? It is
the false Steward that stole his masters daughter.

Laer. This nothings more then matter.

Ophe. There's Rosemary, that's for Remembraunce.
Pray loue remember : and there is Paconcies, that's for
Thoughts.

Laer. A document in madnesse, thoughts & remembrance fitted.

Ophe. There's Fennell for you, and Columbines : ther's
Rew for you, and heere's some for me. Wee may call it
Herbe-Grace a Sundaies : Oh you must weare your Rew
with a difference. There's a Daysie, I would giue you
some Violets, but they wither'd all when my Father dyed : They say, he made a good end ;
For bonny sweet Robin is all my ioy.

Laer. Thought, and Afflliction, Passion, Hell it selfe :
She turnes to Fauour, and to prettinesse.

Ophe. *And will be not come againe,*
And will he not come againe :
No, no, he is dead, go to thy Death-bed,
He neuer wil come againe.
His Beard as white as Snow,
All Flaxen was his Pole :
He is gone, he is gone, and we cast away mone,
Gramercy on his Soule.
And of all Christian Soules, I pray God.
God buy ye.   *Exeunt Ophelia*

Laer. Do you see this, you Gods?

King. *Laertes*, I must common with your greefe,
Or you deny me right: go but apart,

Make choice of whom your wifeft Friends you will,
And they fhall heare and iudge'twixt you and me;
If by direct or by Colaterall hand
They finde vs touch'd, we will our Kingdome giue,
Our Crowne, our Life, and all that we call Ours
To you in fatisfaction. But if not,
Be you content to lend your patience to vs,
And we fhall ioyntly labour with your foule
To giue it due content.

Laer. Let this be fo:
His meanes of death, his obfcure buriall;
No Trophee, Sword, nor Hatchment o're his bones,
No Noble rite, nor formall oftentation,
Cry to be heard, as 'twere from Heauen to Earth,
That I muft call in queftion.

King. So you fhall:
And where th'offence is, let the great Axe fall.
I pray you go with me.   Exeunt

Enter Horatio, with an Attendant.

Hora. What are they that would fpeake with me?
Ser. Saylors fir, they fay they haue Letters for you.
Hor. Let them come in,
I do not know from what part of the world
I fhould be greeted, if not from Lord Hamlet.

Enter Saylor.

Say. God bleffe you Sir.
Hor. Let him bleffe thee too.
Say. Hee fhall Sir, and't.pleafe him. There's a Letter
for you Sir: It comes from th'Ambaffadours that was
bound for England, if your name be Horatio, as I am let
to know it is.

Reads the Letter.

HOratio, *When thou fhalt haue ouerlook'd this, giue thefe
Fellowes fome meanes to the King: They haue Letters
for him. Ere we were two dayes old at Sea, a Pyrate of very
Warlicke appointment gaue vs Chace. Finding our felues too
flow of Saile, we put on a compelled Valour. In the Grapple, I
boorded them: On the inftant they got cleare of our Shippe, fo
I alone became their Prifoner. They haue dealt with mee, like
Theeues of Mercy, but they knew what they did. I am to doe
a good turne for them. Let the King haue the Letters I haue
fent, and repaire thou to me with as much haft as thou wouldeft
flye death. I haue words to fpeake in your eare, will make thee
dumbe, yet are they much too light for the bore of the Matter.
Thefe good Fellowes will bring thee where I am. Rofincrance
and Guildenfterne, hold their courfe for England. Of them
I haue much to tell thee, Farewell.*

                    He that thou knoweft thine,
                              Hamlet.

Come, I will giue you way for thefe your Letters,
And do't the fpeedier, that you may direct me
To him from whom you brought them.   Exit.

Enter King and Laertes.

King. Now muft your confcience my acquittance feal,
And you muft put me in your heart for Friend,
Sith you haue heard, and with a knowing eare,
That he which hath your Noble Father flaine,
Purfued my life.

Laer. It well appeares. But tell me,
Why you proceeded not againft thefe feates,
So crimefull, and fo Capitall in Nature,
As by your Safety, Wifedome, all things elfe,

You mainly were ftirr'd vp?

King. O for two fpeciall Reafons,
Which may to you (perhaps) feeme much vnfinnowed,
And yet to me they are ftrong. The Queen his Mother,
Liues almoft by his lookes: and for my felfe,
My Vertue or my Plague, be it either which,
She's fo coniunctiue to my life and foule;
That as the Starre moues not but in his Sphere,
I could not but by her. The other Motiue,
Why to a publike count I might not go,
Is the great loue the generall gender beare him,
Who dipping all his Faults in their affection,
Would like the Spring that turneth Wood to Stone,
Conuert his Gyues to Graces. So that my Arrowes
Too flightly timbred for fo loud a Winde,
Would haue reuerted to my Bow againe,
And not where I had arm'd them.

Laer. And fo haue I a Noble Father loft,
A Sifter driuen into defperate tearmes,
Who was (if praifes may go backe againe)
Stood Challenger on mount of all the Age
For her perfections. But my reuenge will come.

King. Breake not your fleepes for that,
You muft not thinke
That we are made of ftuffe, fo flat, and dull,
That we can let our Beard be fhooke with danger,
And thinke it paftime. You fhortly fhall heare more,
I lou'd your Father, and we loue our Selfe,
And that I hope will teach you to imagine.———

Enter a Meffenger.

How now? What Newes?
Mef. Letters my Lord from Hamlet. This to your
Maiefty: this to the Queene.
King. From Hamlet? Who brought them?
Mef. Saylors my Lord they fay, I faw them not:
They were giuen me by Claudio, he receiu'd them.
King. Laertes you fhall heare them:
Leaue vs.   Exit Meffenger

High and Mighty, *you fhall know I am fet naked on your
Kingdome. To morrow fhall I begge leaue to fee your Kingly
Eyes. When I fhall (firft asking your Pardon thereunto) re-
count th'Occafions of my fodaine, and more ftrange returne.*
                                        Hamlet.

What fhould this meane? Are all the reft come backe?
Or is it fome abufe? Or no fuch thing?

Laer. Know you the hand?
Kin. 'Tis Hamlets Character', naked and in a Poft-
fcript here he fayes alone: Can you aduife me?

Laer. I'm loft in it my Lord; but let him come,
It warmes the very ficknefle in my heart,
That I fhall liue and tell him to his teeth;
Thus diddeft thou.

Kin. If it be fo Laertes, as how fhould it be fo:
How otherwife will you be rul'd by me?

Laer. If fo you'l not o'rerule me to a peace.
Kin. To thine owne peace: if he be now return'd,
As checking at his Voyage, and that he meanes
No more to vndertake it; I will worke him
To an exployt now ripe in my Deuice,
Vnder the which he fhall not choofe but fall;
And for his death no winde of blame fhall breath,
But euen his Mother fhall vncharge the practice,
And call it accident: Some two Monthes hence
Here was a Gentleman of Normandy,
I'ue feene my felfe, and feru'd againft the French,
And they ran well on Horfebacke; but this Gallant

                                        Had

Had witchcraft in't; he grew into his Seat,
And to such wondrous doing brought his Horse,
As had he beene encorps't and demy-Natur'd
With the braue Beast, so farre he past my thought,
That I in forgery of shapes and trickes,
Come short of what he did.

Laer. A Norman was't?
Kin. A Norman.
Laer. Vpon my life Lamound.
Kin. The very same.
Laer. I know him well, he is the Brooch indeed,
And Iemme of all our Nation.
Kin. Hee mad confession of you,
And gaue you such a Masterly report,
For Art and exercise in your defence;
And for your Rapier most especially,
That he cryed out, t'would be a sight indeed,
If one could match you Sir. This report of his
Did Hamlet so envenom with his Enuy,
That he could nothing doe but wish and begge,
Your sodaine comming ore to play with him;
Now out of this.

Laer. Why out of this, my Lord?
Kin. Laertes was your Father deare to you?
Or are you like the painting of a sorrow,
A face without a heart?

Laer. Why aske you this?
Kin. Not that I thinke you did not loue your Father,
But that I know Loue is begun by Time:
And that I see in passages of proofe,
Time qualifies the sparke and fire of it:
Hamlet comes backe: what would you vndertake,
To show your selfe your Fathers sonne indeed,
More then in words?

Laer. To cut his throat i'th' Church.
Kin. No place indeed should murder Sancturize;
Reuenge should haue no bounds: but good Laertes
Will you doe this, keepe close within your Chamber,
Hamlet return'd, shall know you are come home:
Wee'l put on those shall praise your excellence,
And set a double varnish on the fame
The Frenchman gaue you, bring you in fine together,
And wager on your heads, he being remisse,
Most generous, and free from all contriuing,
Will not peruse the Foiles? So that with ease,
Or with a little shuffling, you may choose
A Sword vnbaited, and in a passe of practice,
Requit him for your Father.

Laer. I will doo't,
And for that purpose Ile annoint my Sword:
I bought an Vnction of a Mountebanke
So mortall, I but dipt a knife in it,
Where it drawes blood, no Cataplasme so rare,
Collected from all Simples that haue Vertue
Vnder the Moone, can saue the thing from death,
That is but scratcht withall: Ile touch my point,
With this contagion, that if I gall him slightly,
I t may be death.

Kin Let's further thinke of this,
Weigh what conuenience both of time and meanes
May fit vs to our shape, if this should faile;
And that our drift looke through our bad performance,
'Twere better not assaid; therefore this Proiect
Should haue a backe or second, that might hold,
If this should blast in proofe: Soft, let me see
Wee'l make a solemne wager on your commings,

I ha't: when in your motion you are hot and dry,
As make your bowts more violent to the end,
And that he cals for drinke; Ile haue prepar'd him
A Challice for the nonce; whereon but sipping,
If he by chance escape your venom'd stuck,
Our purpose may hold there; how sweet Queene.

Enter Queene.
Queen. One woe doth tread vpon anothers heele,
So fast they'l follow: your Sister's drown'd Laertes.
Laer. Drown'd! O where?
Queen. There is a Willow growes aslant a Brooke,
That shewes his hore leaues in the glassie streame:
There with fantasticke Garlands did she come,
Of Crow-flowers, Nettles, Dayses, and long Purples,
That liberall Shepheards giue a grosser name;
But our cold Maids doe Dead Mens Fingers call them:
There on the pendant boughes, her Coronet weeds
Clambring to hang; an enuious sliuer broke,
When downe the weedy Trophies, and her selfe,
Fell in the weeping Brooke, her cloathes spred wide,
And Mermaid-like, a while they bore her vp,
Which time she chaunted snatches of old tunes,
As one incapable of her owne distresse,
Or like a creature Natiue, and indued
Vnto that Element: but long it could not be,
Till that her garments, heauy with her drinke,
Pul'd the poore wretch from her melodious buy,
To muddy death.

Laer. Alas then, is she drown'd?
Queen. Drown'd, drown'd.
Laer. Too much of water hast thou poore Ophelia,
And therefore I forbid my teares: but yet
It is our tricke, Nature her custome holds,
Let shame say what it will; when these are gone
The woman will be out: Adue my Lord,
I haue a speech of fire, that faine would blaze,
But that this folly doubts it. Exit.

Kin. Let's follow, Gertrude:
How much I had to doe to calme his rage?
Now feare I this will giue it start againe;
Therefore let's follow. Exeunt.

Enter two Clownes.
Clown. Is she to bee buried in Christian buriall, that wilfully seekes her owne saluation?
Other. I tell thee she is, and therefore make her Graue straight, the Crowner hath sate on her, and finds it Christian buriall.
Clo. How can that be, vnlesse she drowned her selfe in her owne defence?
Other. Why 'tis found so.
Clo. It must be Se offendendo, it cannot bee else: for heere lies the point; If I drowne my selfe wittingly, it argues an Act: and an Act hath three branches. It is an Act to doe and to performe; argall she drown'd her selfe wittingly.
Other. Nay but heare you Goodman Deluer.
Clown. Giue me leaue; heere lies the water; good: heere stands the man; good: If the man goe to this water and drowne himsele; it is will he, nill he, he goes; marke you that? But if the water come to him & drowne him; hee drownes not himselfe. Argall, hee that is not guilty of his owne death, shortens not his owne life.
Other. But is this law?
Clo. I marry is't, Crowners Quest Law.

Other

Other. Will you ha the truth on't: if this had not beene a Gentlewoman, shee should haue beene buried out of Christian Buriall.

Clo. Why there thou say'st. And the more pitty that great folke should haue countenance in this world to drowne or hang themselues, more then their euen Christian. Come, my Spade; there is no ancient Gentlemen, but Gardiners, Ditchers and Graue-makers; they hold vp *Adams* Profession.

Other. Was he a Gentleman?

Clo. He was the first that euer bore Armes.

Other. Why he had none.

Clo. What, ar't a Heathen? how dost thou vnderstand the Scripture? the Scripture sayes *Adam* dig'd; could hee digge without Armes? Ile put another question to thee; if thou answerest me not to the purpose, confesse thy selfe———

Other. Go too.

Clo. What is he that builds stronger then either the Mason, the Shipwright, or the Carpenter?

Other. The Gallowes maker; for that Frame outliues a thousand Tenants.

Clo. I like thy wit well in good faith, the Gallowes does well; but how does it well? it does well to those that doe ill: now, thou dost ill to say the Gallowes is built stronger then the Church: Argall, the Gallowes may doe well to thee. Too't againe, Come.

Other. Who builds stronger then a Mason, a Shipwright, or a Carpenter?

Clo. I, tell me that, and vnyoake.

Other. Marry, now I can tell.

Clo. Too't.

Other. Masse, I cannot tell.

Enter Hamlet and Horatio a farre off.

Clo. Cudgell thy braines no more about it; for your dull Asse will not mend his pace with beating, and when you are ask't this question next, say a Graue-maker: the Houses that he makes, lasts till Doomesday: go, get thee to *Yaughan*, fetch me a stoupe of Liquor.

Sings.

In youth when I did loue, did loue,
 me thought it was very sweete:
To contract O the time for a my behoue,
 O me thought there was nothing meete.

Ham. Ha's this fellow no feeling of his businesse, that he sings at Graue-making?

Hor. Custome hath made it in him a property of easinesse.

Ham. 'Tis ee'n so; the hand of little Imployment hath the daintier sense.

Clowne sings.

But Age with his stealing steps
 hath caught me in his clutch:
And hath shipped me intill the Land,
 as if I had neuer beene such.

Ham. That Scull had a tongue in it, and could sing once: how the knaue iowles it to th' grownd, as if it were *Caines* Iaw-bone, that did the first murther: It might be the Pate of a Politician which this Asse o're Offices: one that could circumuent God, might it not?

Hor. It might, my Lord.

Ham. Or of a Courtier, which could say, Good Morrow sweet Lord: how dost thou, good Lord? this might be my Lord such a one, that prais'd my Lord such a ones Horse, when he meant to begge it; might it not?

Hor. I, my Lord.

Ham. Why ee'n so: and now my Lady Wormes, Chaplesse, and knockt about the Mazard with a Sextons Spade; heere's fine Reuolution, if wee had the tricke to see't. Did these bones cost no more the breeding, but to play at Loggets with 'em? mine ake to thinke on't.

Clowne sings.

A Pickhaxe and a Spade, a Spade,
 for and a shrowding-Sheete:
O a Pit of Clay for to be made,
 for such a Guest is meete.

Ham. There's another: why might not that bee the Scull of of a Lawyer? where be his Quiddits now? his Quillets? his Cases? his Tenures, and his Tricks? why doe's he suffer this rude knaue now to knocke him about the Sconce with a dirty Shouell, and will not tell him of his Action of Battery? hum. This fellow might be in's time a great buyer of Land, with his Statutes, his Recognizances, his Fines, his double Vouchers, his Recoueries: Is this the fine of his Fines, and the recouery of his Recoueries, to haue his fine Pate full of fine Dirt? will his Vouchers vouch him no more of his Purchases, and double ones too, then the length and breadth of a paire of Indentures? the very Conueyances of his Lands will hardly lye in this Boxe; and must the Inheritor himselfe haue no more? ha?

Hor. Not a iot more, my Lord.

Ham. Is not Parchment made of Sheep-skinnes?

Hor. I my Lord, and of Calue-skinnes too.

Ham. They are Sheepe and Calues that seek out assurance in that. I will speake to this fellow: whose Graue's this Sir?

Clo. Mine Sir:

O a Pit of Clay for to be made,
 for such a Guest is meete.

Ham. I thinke it be thine indeed: for thou liest in't.

Clo. You lye out on't Sir, and therefore it is not yours: for my part, I doe not lye in't; and yet it is mine.

Ham. Thou dost lye in't, to be in't and say 'tis thine: 'tis for the dead, not for the quicke, therefore thou lyest.

Clo. 'Tis a quicke lye Sir, 'twill away againe from me to you.

Ham. What man dost thou digge it for?

Clo. For no man Sir.

Ham. What woman then?

Clo. For none neither.

Ham. Who is to be buried in't?

Clo. One that was a woman Sir; but rest her Soule, shee's dead.

Ham. How absolute the knaue is? wee must speake by the Carde, or equiuocation will vndoe vs: by the Lord *Horatio*, these three yeares I haue taken note of it, the Age is growne so picked, that the toe of the Pesant comes so neere the heeles of our Courtier, hee galls his Kibe. How long hast thou been a Graue-maker?

Clo. Of all the dayes i'th' yeare, I came too't that day that our last King *Hamlet* o'recame *Fortinbras.*

Ham. How long is that since?

Clo. Cannot you tell that? euery foole can tell that: It was the very day, that young *Hamlet* was borne, hee that was mad, and sent into England.

Ham. I marry, why was he sent into England?

Clo. Why, because he was mad; hee shall recouer his wits there; or if he do not, it's no great matter there.

Ham.

Ham. Why?

Clo. 'Twill not be seene in him, there the men are as mad as he.

Ham. How came he mad?

Clo. Very strangely they say.

Ham. How strangely?

Clo. Faith e'ene with loosing his wits.

Ham. Vpon what ground?

Clo. Why heere in Denmarke: I haue bin sixteene heere, man and Boy thirty yeares.

Ham. How long will a man lie 'ith' earth ere he rot?

Clo. Ifaith, if he be not rotten before he die (as we haue many pocky Coarses now adaies, that will scarce hold the laying in) he will last you some eight yeare, or nine yeare. A Tanner will last you nine yeare.

Ham. Why he, more then another?

Clo. Why sir, his hide is so tan'd with his Trade, that he will keepe out water a great while. And your water, is a sore Decayer of your horson dead body. Heres a Scull now: this Scul, has laine in the earth three & twenty years.

Ham. Whose was it?

Clo. A whoreson mad Fellowes it was; Whose doe you thinke it was?

Ham. Nay, I know not.

Clo. A pestlence on him for a mad Rogue, a pou'rd a Flaggon of Renish on my head once. This same Scull Sir, this same Scull sir, was *Yoricks* Scull, the Kings Iester.

Ham. This?

Clo. E'ene that.

Ham. Let me see. Alas poore *Yorick*, I knew him *Horatio*, a fellow of infinite Iest; of most excellent fancy, he hath borne me on his backe a thousand times: And how abhorred my Imagination is, my gorge rises at it. Heere hung those lipps, that I haue kist I know not how oft. VVhere be your Iibes now? Your Gambals? Your Songs? Your flashes of Merriment that were wont to set the Table on a Rore? No one now to mock your own Ieering? Quite chopfalne? Now get you to my Ladies Chamber, and tell her, let her paint an inch thicke, to this fauour she must come. Make her laugh at that: prythee *Horatio* tell me one thing.

Hor. What's that my Lord?

Ham. Dost thou thinke *Alexander* lookt o'this fashion i'th' earth?

Hor. E'ene so.

Ham. And smelt so? Puh.

Hor. E'ene so, my Lord.

Ham. To what base vses we may returne *Horatio*. Why may not Imagination trace the Noble dust of *Alexander*, till he find it stopping a bunghole.

Hor. 'Twere to consider: to curiously to consider so.

Ham. No faith, not a iot. But to follow him thether with modestie enough, & likeliehood to lead it; as thus. *Alexander* died: *Alexander* was buried: *Alexander* returneth into dust; the dust is earth; of earth we make Lome, and why of that Lome (whereto he was conuerted) might they not stopp a Beere-barrell?
Imperiall *Cæsar*, dead and turn'd to clay,
Might stop a hole to keepe the winde away.
Oh, that that earth, which kept the world in awe,
Should patch a Wall, t'expell the winters flaw.
But soft, but soft, aside; heere comes the King.

Enter King, Queene, Laertes, and a Coffin, with Lords attendant.

The Queene, the Courtiers. Who is that they follow,

And with such maimed rites? This doth betoken,
The Coarse they follow, did with disperate hand,
Fore do it owne life; 'twas some Estate.
Couch we a while, and mark.

Laer. What Cerimony else?

Ham. That is *Laertes*, a very Noble youth: Marke.

Laer. What Cerimony else?

Priest. Her Obsequies haue bin as farre inlarg'd,
As we haue warrantis, her death was doubtfull,
And but that great Command, o're-swaies the order,
She should in ground vnsanctified haue lodg'd,
Till the last Trumpet. For charitable praier,
Shardes, Flints, and Peebles, should be throwne on her:
Yet heere she is allowed her Virgin Rites,
Her Maiden strewments, and the bringing home
Of Bell and Buriall.

Laer. Must there no more be done?

Priest. No more be done:
We should prophane the seruice of the dead,
To sing sage *Requiem*, and such rest to her
As to peace-parted Soules.

Laer. Lay her i'th' earth,
And from her faire and vnpolluted flesh,
May Violets spring. I tell thee (churlish Priest)
A Ministring Angell shall my Sister be,
When thou liest howling?

Ham. What, the faire *Ophelia*?

Queene. Sweets, to the sweet farewell.
I hop'd thou should'st haue bin my *Hamlets* wife:
I thought thy Bride-bed to haue deckt (sweet Maid)
And not t'haue strew'd thy Graue.

Laer. Oh terrible woer,
Fall ten times trebble, on that cursed head
Whose wicked deed, thy most Ingenious sence
Depriu'd thee of. Hold off the earth a while,
Till I haue caught her once more in mine armes:

Leaps in the graue.

Now pile your dust, vpon the quicke, and dead,
Till of this flat a Mountaine you haue made,
To o're top old *Pelion*, or the skyish head
Of blew *Olympus*.

Ham. What is he, whose griefes
Beares such an Emphasis? whose phrase of Sorrow
Coniure the wandring Starres, and makes them stand
Like wonder-wounded hearers? This is I,
Hamlet the Dane.

Laer. The deuill take thy soule.

Ham. Thou prai'st not well,
I prythee take thy fingers from my throat;
Sir though I am not Spleenatiue, and rash,
Yet haue I something in me dangerous,
Which let thy wisenesse feare. Away thy hand.

King. Pluck them asunder.

Qu. Hamlet, Hamlet.

Gen. Good my Lord be quiet.

Ham. Why I will fight with him vppon this Theme,
Vntill my eielids will no longer wag.

Qu. Oh my Sonne, what Theame?

Ham. I lou'd *Ophelia*; fortie thousand Brothers
Could not (with all there quantitie of Loue)
Make vp my summe. What wilt thou do for her?

King. Oh he is mad *Laertes*,

Qu. For loue of God forbeare him.

Ham. Come show me what thou'lt doe.
Woo't weepe? Woo't fight? Woo't teare thy selfe?
Woo't drinke vp *Esile*, eate a Crocodile?

Ile

Ile doo't. Doſt thou come heere to whine;
To outface me with leaping in her Graue?
Be buried quicke with her, and ſo will I.
And if thou prate of Mountaines; let them throw
Millions of Akers on vs; till our ground
Sindging his pate againſt the burning Zone,
Make *Oſſa* like a wart. Nay, and thou't mouth,
Ile rant as well as thou.

Kin. This is meere Madneſſe:
And thus awhile the fit will worke on him:
Anon as patient as the female Doue,
When that her golden Cuplet are diſclos'd;
His ſilence will ſit drooping.

Ham. Heare you Sir:
What is the reaſon that you vſe me thus?
I loud' you euer; but it is no matter:
Let *Hercules* himſelfe doe what he may,
The Cat will Mew, and Dogge will haue his day. *Exit.*

Kin. I pray you good *Horatio* wait vpon him,
Strengthen you patience in our laſt nights ſpeech,
Wee'l put the matter to the preſent puſh:
Good *Gertrude* ſet ſome watch ouer your Sonne,
This Graue ſhall haue a liuing Monument:
An houre of quiet ſhortly ſhall we ſee;
Till then, in patience our proceeding be.   *Exeunt.*

Enter Hamlet and Horatio.

Ham. So much for this Sir; now let me ſee the other,
You doe remember all the Circumſtance.

Hor. Remember it my Lord?

Ham. Sir, in my heart there was a kinde of fighting,
That would not let me ſleepe; me thought I lay
Worſe then the mutines in the Bilboes, raſhly,
(And praiſe be raſhneſſe for it) let vs know,
Our indiſcretion ſometimes ſerues vs well,
When our deare plots do paule, and that ſhould teach vs,
There's a Diuinity that ſhapes our ends,
Rough-hew them how we will.

Hor. That is moſt certaine.

Ham. Vp from my Cabin
My ſea-gowne ſcarft about me in the darke,
Grop'd I to finde out them; had my deſire,
Finger'd their Packet, and in fine, withdrew
To mine owne roome againe, making ſo bold,
(My feares forgetting manners) to vnſeale
Their grand Commiſſion, where I found *Horatio*,
Oh royall knauery: An exact command,
Larded with many ſeuerall ſorts of reaſon;
Importing Denmarks health, and Englands too,
With hoo, ſuch Bugges and Goblins in my life,
That on the ſuperuize no leaſure bated,
No not to ſtay the grinding of the Axe,
My head ſhoud be ſtruck off.

Hor. Iſt poſſible?

Ham. Here's the Commiſſion, read it at more leyſure:
But wilt thou heare me how I did proceed?

Hor. I beſeech you.

Ham. Being thus benetted round with Villaines,
Ere I could make a Prologue to my braines,
They had begun the Play. I ſate me downe,
Deuis'd a new Commiſſion, wrote it faire,
I once did hold it as our Statiſts doe,
A baſeneſſe to write faire; and laboured much
How to forget that learning: but Sir now,
It did me Yeomans ſeruice: wilt thou know
The effects of what I wrote?

Hor. I, good my Lord.

Ham. An earneſt Coniuration from the King,
As England was his faithfull Tributary,
As loue betweene them, as the Palme ſhould flouriſh,
As Peace ſhould ſtill her wheaten Garland weare,
And ſtand a Comma 'tweene their amities,
And many ſuch like Aſſis of great charge,
That on the view and know of theſe Contents,
Without debatement further, more or leſſe,
He ſhould the bearers put to ſodaine death,
Not ſhriuing time allowed.

Hor. How was this ſeal'd?

Ham. Why, euen in that was Heauen ordinate;
I had my fathers Signet in my Purſe,
Which was the Modell of that Daniſh Seale:
Folded the Writ vp in forme of the other,
Subſcrib'd it, gau't th'impreſſion, plac't it ſafely,
The changeling neuer knowne: Now, the next day
Was our Sea Fight, and what to this was ſement,
Thou know'ſt already.

Hor. So *Guildenſterne* and *Roſincrance*, go too't.

Ham. Why man, they did make loue to this imployment
They are not neere my Conſcience; their debate
Doth by their owne inſinuation grow:
'Tis dangerous, when the baſer nature comes
Betweene the paſſe, and fell incenſed points
Of mighty oppoſites.

Hor. Why, what a King is this?

Ham. Does it not, thinkſt thee, ſtand me now vpon
He that hath kil'd my King, and whor'd my Mother,
Popt in betweene th'election and my hopes,
Throwne out his Angle for my proper life,
And with ſuch coozenage; is't not perfect conſcience,
To quit him with this arme? And is't not to be damn'd
To let this Canker of our nature come
In further euill.

Hor. It muſt be ſhortly knowne to him from England
What is the iſſue of the buſineſſe there.

Ham. It will be ſhort,
The *interim's* mine, and a mans life's no more
Then to ſay one: but I am very ſorry good *Horatio*,
That to *Laertes* I forgot my ſelfe;
For by the image of my Cauſe, I ſee
The Portraiture of his; Ile count his fauours:
But ſure the brauery of his griefe did put me
Into a Towring paſſion.

Hor. Peace, who comes heere?

Enter young Oſricke.   (marke.

Oſr. Your Lordſhip is right welcome back to Den-

Ham. I humbly thank you Sir, doſt know this waterflie?

Hor. No my good Lord.

Ham. Thy ſtate is the more gracious; for 'tis a vice to
know him: he hath much Land, and fertile; let a Beaſt
be Lord of Beaſts, and his Crib ſhall ſtand at the Kings
Meſſe; 'tis a Chowgh; but as I ſaw ſpacious in the poſ-
ſeſſion of dirt.

Oſr. Sweet Lord, if your friendſhip were at leyſure,
I ſhould impart a thing to you from his Maieſty.

Ham. I will receiue it with all diligence of ſpirit, put
your Bonet to his right vſe, 'tis for the head.

Oſr. I thanke your Lordſhip, 'tis very hot.

Ham. No, beleeue mee 'tis very cold, the winde is
Northerly.

Oſr. It is indifferent cold my Lord indeed.

Ham. Mee thinkes it is very ſoultry, and hot for my
Complexion.

Ofr. Exceedingly,my Lord,it is very foultry,as 'twere
I cannot tell how: but my Lord,his Maiefty bad me fig-
nifie to you, that he ha's laid a great wager on your head:
Sir, this is the matter.

Ham. I befeech you remember.

Ofr. Nay,in good faith, for mine eafe in good faith :
Sir,you are not ignorant of what excellence *Laertes* is at
his weapon.

Ham. What's his weapon?

Ofr. Rapier and dagger.

Ham. That's two of his weapons; but well.

Ofr. The fir King ha's wag'd with him fix Barbary Hor-
fes, againft the which he impon'd as I take it, fixe French
Rapiers and Poniards , with their affignes, as Girdle,
Hangers or fo: three of the Carriages infaith are very
deare to fancy,very refponfiue to the hilts, moft delicate
carriages, and of very liberall conceit.

Ham. What call you the Carriages?

Ofr. The Carriages Sir, are the hangers.

Ham. The phrafe would bee more Germaine to the
matter : If we could carry Cannon by our fides; I would
it might be Hangers till then; but on fixe Barbary Hor-
fes againft fixe French Swords: their Affignes,and three
liberall conceited Carriages , that's the French but a-
gainft the Danifh; why is this impon'd as you call it?

Ofr. The King Sir,hath laid that in a dozen paffes betweene you and him, hee fhall not exceed you three hits;
He hath one twelue for mine, and that would come to
imediate tryall, if your Lordfhip would vouchfafe the
Anfwere.

Ham. How if I anfwere no?

Ofr. I meane my Lord, the oppofition of your perfon
in tryall.

Ham. Sir, I will walke heere in the Hall; if it pleafe
his Maieftie, 'tis the breathing time of day with me; let
the Foyles bee brought, the Gentleman willing, and the
King hold his purpofe; I will win for him if I can: if
not, Ile gaine nothing but my fhame, and the odde hits.

Ofr. Shall I redeliuer you ee'n fo?

Ham. To this effect Sir, after what flourifh your nature will.

Ofr. I commend my duty to your Lordfhip.

Ham. Yours, yours; hee does well to commend it
himfelfe, there are no tongues elfe for's tongue.

Hor. This Lapwing runs away with the fhell on his
head.

Ham. He did Complie with his Dugge before hee
fuck't it: thus had he and mine more of the fame Beauy
that I know the droffie age dotes on;only got the tune of
the time , and outward habite of encounter, a kinde of
yefty collection, which carries them through & through
the moft fond and winnowed opinions;and doe but blow
them to their tryalls: the Bubbles are out.

Hor. You will lofe this wager,my Lord.

Ham. I doe not thinke fo, fince he went into France,
I haue beene in continuall practice; I fhall winne at the
oddes : but thou wouldeft not thinke how all heere a-
bout my heart: but it is no matter.

Hor. Nay, good my Lord.

Ham. It is but foolery; but it is fuch a kinde of
gain-giuing as would perhaps trouble a woman.

Hor. If your minde diflike any thing,obey.I will fore-
ftall their repaire hither, and fay you are not fit.

Ham. Not a whit, we defie Augury; there's a fpeciall
Prouidence in the fall of a fparrow. If it be now, 'tis not
to come : if it beenot to come, it will bee now : if it

be not now; yet it will come; the readineffe is all,fince no
man ha's ought of what he leaues. What is't to leaue be-
times?

Enter *King, Queene, Laertes and Lords, with other Atten-
dants with Foyles, and Gauntlets, a Table and
Flagons of Wine on it.*

Kin. Come *Hamlet*,come,and take this hand from me.

Ham. Giue me your pardon Sir,I'ue done you wrong,
But pardon't as you are a Gentleman.
This prefence knowes,
And you muft needs haue heard how I am punifht
With fore diftraction ? What I haue done
That might your nature honour,and exception
Roughly awake, I heere proclaime was madneffe :
Was't *Hamlet* wrong'd *Laertes* ? Neuer *Hamlet*.
If *Hamlet* from himfelfe be tane away :
And when he's not himfelfe,do's wrong *Laertes*,
Then *Hamlet* does it not, *Hamlet* denies it :
Who does it then? His Madneffe ? If't be fo,
Hamlet is of the Faction that is wrong'd,
His madneffe is poore *Hamlets* Enemy.
Sir, in this Audience,
Let my difclaiming from a purpos'd euill,
Free me fo farre in your moft generous thoughts,
That I haue fhot mine Arrow o're the houfe,
And hurt my Mother.

Laer. I am fatisfied in Nature,
Whofe motiue in this cafe fhould ftirre me moft
To my Reuenge. But in my termes of Honor
I ftand aloofe, and will no reconcilement,
Till by fome elder Mafters of knowne Honor,
I haue a voyce, and prefident of peace
To keepe my name vngorg'd. But till that time,
I do receiue your offer'd loue like loue,
And wil not wrong it.

Ham. I do embrace it freely,
And will this Brothers wager frankely play.
Giue vs the Foyles : Come on.

Laer. Come one for me.

Ham. Ile be your foile *Laertes*,in mine ignorance,
Your Skill fhall like a Starre i'th'darkeft night,
Sticke fiery off indeede.

Laer. You mocke me Sir.

Ham. No by this hand.

King. Giue them the Foyles yong *Ofricke*,
Coufen *Hamlet*, you know the wager.

Ham. Verie well my Lord,
Your Grace hath laide the oddes a'th'weaker fide.

King. I do not feare it,
I haue feene you both :
But fince he is better'd,we haue therefore oddes.

Laer. This is too heauy,
Let me fee another.

Ham. This likes me well,
Thefe Foyles haue all a length.   *Prepare to play.*

Ofricke. I my good Lord.

King. Set me the Stopes of wine vpon that Table :
If *Hamlet* giue the firft, or fecond hit,
Or quit in anfwer of the third exchange,
Let all the Battlements their Ordinance fire,
The King fhal drinke to *Hamlets* better breath,
And in the Cup an vnion fhal he throw
Richer then that, which foure fucceffiue Kings
In Denmarkes Crowne haue worne.

Giue

Giue me the Cups,
And let the Kettle to the Trumpets speake,
The Trumpet to the Cannoneer without,
The Cannons to the Heauens, the Heauen to Earth,
Now the King drinkes to *Hamlet.* Come, begin,
And you the Iudges beare a wary eye.

 Ham. Come on fir.
 Laer. Come on fir.   *They play.*
 Ham. One.
 Laer. No.
 Ham. Iudgement.
 Ofr. A hit, a very palpable hit.
 Laer. Well : againe.
 King. Stay, giue me drinke.
Hamlet, this Pearle is thine,
Here's to thy health. Giue him the cup,
     Trumpets found, and shot goes off.
 Ham. Ile play this bout first, set by a-while.
Come : Another hit ; what fay you ?
 Laer. A touch, a touch, I do confeffe.
 King. Our Sonne shall win.
 Qu. He's fat, and scant of breath.
Heere's a Napkin, rub thy browes,
The Queene Carowfes to thy fortune, *Hamlet.*
 Ham. Good Madam.
 King. *Gertrude,* do not drinke.
 Qu. I will my Lord ;
I pray you pardon me.
 King. It is the poyson'd Cup, it is too late.
 Ham. I dare not drinke yet Madam,
By and by.
 Qu. Come, let me wipe thy face.
 Laer. My Lord, Ile hit him now.
 King. I do not thinke't.
 Laer. And yet 'tis almoft 'gainft my confcience.
 Ham. Come, for the third.
Laertes, you but dally,
I pray you paffe with your beft violence,
I am affear'd you make a wanton of me.
 Laer. Say you fo ? Come on.   *Play.*
 Ofr. Nothing neither way.
 Laer. Haue at you now.
    In fcuffling they change Rapiers.
 King. Part them, they are incens'd.
 Ham. Nay come, againe.
 Ofr. Looke to the Queene there hoa.
 Hor. They bleed on both fides. How is't my Lord ?
 Ofr. How is't *Laertes* ?
 Laer. Why as a Woodcocke
To mine Sprindge, *Ofricke,*
I am iuftly kill'd with mine owne Treacherie.
 Ham. How does the Queene ?
 King. She founds to fee them bleede.
 Qu. No, no, the drinke, the drinke,
Oh my deere *Hamlet,* the drinke, the drinke,
I am poyson'd.
 Ham. Oh Villany ! How ? Let the doore be lock'd,
Treacherie, feeke it out.
 Laer. It is heere *Hamlet.*
Hamlet, thou art flaine,
No Medicine in the world can do thee good.
In thee, there is not halfe an houre of life ;
The Treacherous Inftrument is in thy hand,
Vnbated and envenom'd : the foule practife
Hath turn'd it felfe on me. Loe, heere I lye,
Neuer to rife againe : Thy Mothers poyson'd :

I can no more, the King, the King's too blame.
 Ham. The point envenom'd too,
Then venome to thy worke.
        Hurts the King.
 All. Treafon, Treafon.
 King. O yet defend me Friends, I am but hurt.
 Ham. Heere thou inceftuous, murdrous,
Damned Dane,
Drinke off this Potion : Is thy Vnion heere ?
Follow my Mother.   *King Dyes.*
 Laer. He is iuftly feru'd.
It is a poyson temp'red by himfelfe :
Exchange forgiueneffe with me, Noble *Hamlet ;*
Mine and my Fathers death come not vpon thee,
Nor thine on me.   *Dyes.*
 Ham. Heauen make thee free of it, I follow thee.
I am dead *Horatio,* wretched Queene adiew,
You that looke pale, and tremble at this chance,
That are but Mutes or audience to this acte :
Had I but time (as this fell Sergeant death
Is ftrick'd in his Arreft) oh I could tell you.
But let it be : *Horatio,* I am dead,
Thou liu'ft, report me and my caufes right
To the vnfatisfied.
 Hor. Neuer beleeue it.
I am more an Antike Roman then a Dane:
Heere's yet fome Liquor left.
 Ham. As th'art a man, giue me the Cup.
Let go, by Heauen Ile haue't.
Oh good *Horatio,* what a wounded name,
(Things ftanding thus vnknowne) shall liue behind me.
If thou did'ft euer hold me in thy heart,
Abfent thee from felicitie awhile,
And in this harfh world draw thy breath in paine,
To tell my Storie.
     March afarre off, and shout within.
What warlike noyfe is this ?

      Enter Ofricke.
 Ofr. Yong *Fortinbras,* with conqueft come frō Poland
To th'Ambaffadors of England giues this warlike volly.
 Ham. O I dye *Horatio :*
The potent poyson quite ore-crowes my fpirit,
I cannot liue to heare the Newes from England,
But I do prophefie th'election lights
On *Fortinbras,* he ha's my dying voyce,
So tell him with the occurrents more and leffe,
Which haue folicited. The reft is filence. O, o, o, o. *Dyes*
 Hora. Now cracke a Noble heart :
Goodnight fweet Prince,
And flights of Angels fing thee to thy reft,
Why do's the Drumme come hither ?

Enter Fortinbras and English Ambaffador, with Drumme,
     Colours, and Attendants.
 Fortin. Where is this fight ?
 Hor. What is it ye would fee ;
If ought of woe, or wonder, ceafe your fearch.
 For. His quarry cries on hauocke. Oh proud death,
What feaft is toward in thine eternall Cell.
That thou fo many Princes, at a fhoote,
So bloodily haft ftrooke.
 Amb. The fight is difmall,
And our affaires from England come too late,
The eares are fenfeleffe that fhould giue vs hearing,
To tell him his command'ment is fulfill'd,

          That

That *Rofincrance* and *Guildenfterne* are dead :
Where fhould we haue our thankes ?
    Hor. Not from his mouth,
Had it th'abilitie of life to thanke you :
He neuer gaue command'ment for their death.
But fince fo iumpe vpon this bloodie queftion,
You from the Polake warres, and you from England
Are heere arriued. Giue order that thefe bodies
High on a ftage be placed to the view,
And let me fpeake to th'yet vnknowing world,
How thefe things came about. So fhall you heare
Of carnall, bloudie, and vnnaturall acts,
Of accidentall iudgements, cafuall flaughters
Of death's put on by cunning, and forc'd caufe,
And in this vpfhot, purpofes miftooke,
Falne on the Inuentors heads. All this can I
Truly deliuer.
    For. Let vs haft to heare it,
And call the Nobleft to the Audience.
For me, with forrow, I embrace my Fortune,
I haue fome Rites of memory in this Kingdome,
Which are ro claime, my vantage doth
Inuite me,
    Hor. Of that I fhall haue alwayes caufe to fpeake,
And from his mouth
Whofe voyce will draw on more :
But let this fame be prefently perform'd,
Euen whiles mens mindes are wilde,
Left more mifchance
On plots, and errors happen.
    For. Let foure Captaines
Beare *Hamlet* like a Soldier to the Stage,
For he was likely, had he beene put on
To haue prou'd moft royally :
And for his paffage,
The Souldiours Muficke, and the rites of Warre
Speake lowdly for him.
Take vp the body ; Such a fight as this
Becomes the Field, but heere fhewes much amis.
Go, bid the Souldiers fhoote.
    Exeunt Marching : after the which, a Peale of
        Ordenance are fhot off.

FINIS.

Selected Variants in Folio *Hamlet* vs. Q2

Plot elements are indicated at the left

Initial lines in each scene of Folio text are indicated in red type.

Selected passages that are unique to Q2 vs. Folio *Hamlet* are indicated on red background.

TLN	Plot element	Initial lines / variant passages	Act·Scene	Q2 line
2900	Laertes discovers Ophelia's madness			2900
		Hora. What are they that,…	IV vi	2973
3000	Hamlet returns, having defeated King's spies; King and Laertes conspire in general terms	*King.* Now must your…	IV vii	3000
				3007
3100	King plans fencing match: Laertes in collusion	Laertes offers to be *organ* of Hamlet's demise		3100
		King's further manipulation of Laertes		3190
3200	Queen announces Ophilia's drowning; Gravediggers prepare grave; Horatio and Hamlet converse with gravediggers	*Clown.* Is she to bee buried…	V i	3200
3300	Scene with grave diggers - *Alas poor Yorick*			3300
3400	Ophelia's funeral procession arrives; Hamlet and Laertes confrontation and struggle			3400
3500	Hamlet tells of escape…*divinity that shapes our ends*	*Ham.* So much for this Sir…	V ii	3500
		Is't not to be damned / to Laertes I forgot my self		3500
3600	Osric announces invitation to fencing match	Hamlet's derision of Osric and Laertes; Queen's request Hamlet reconciliation with Laertes		3600
3700	Fencing begins, Queen drinks from cup; Laertes and Hamlet both cut with poisoned foil; Queen dies / Laertes confesses			3700
3800	Hamlet kills King; Hamlet and Laertes exchange forgiveness; Dying Hamlet to Horatio: Live and tell story; Young Fortinbras returns / claims kingdom			3800
3900				3900

The *Text Graphic of Shakespeare's Hamlet©* was designed and developed by Charles Adams Kelly. Downloads available at HowlandResearch.com. Act and Scene numbers are from the 1865 Globe edition. The TLN or Through Line Numbers were originally used in *The Norton Facsimile: The First Folio of Shakespeare*, copyright © 1968 by W. W. Norton & Company, Inc., and are reproduced by permission.

Hamlet Timeline Chart

Line	Act/Scene	Quote
1600	III i	*King.* And can you by no drift…
1700		
1800	III ii	*Ham.* Speake the Speech…
1900		
2000		
2100		
2200		
2300	III iii	*King.* I like him not…
2400	III iv	*Pol.* He will come straight:
2500		
2600	IV i	*King.* There's matters in…
	IV ii	*Ham.* Safely stowed.
	IV iii	*King.* I have sent to seeke him…
2700	IV iv	*For.* Go Captaine…
2800	IV v	*Qu.* I will not speake with her.

Middle column line references: 1600, 1648, 1700, 1800, 1849, 1900, 2000, 2100, 2200, 2272, 2300, 2375, 2400, 2500, 2587, 2600, 2631, 2662, 2700, 2735, 2745, 2800

Hamlet states his distrust of R & G

Scn. with Norwegian Captn and How all occasions

Events

Line	Event
1600	Hamlet soliloquy - *Oh what a rogue* / Plan to stage a play to test King's guilt
1700	Hamlet soliloquy - *To be or not to be* / Hamlet to Ophelia - Nunnery scene
1800	Hamlet lectures players on techniques
1900	If King shows no guilt, *it is a damned ghost*
2000	Court gathers and play begins
2100	King's reaction to play confirms King's guilt
2200	Hamlet requested to meet with Queen
2300	King advises of plan to send Hamlet to England / Polonius plans to hide behind the arras / Hamlet's chance to kill King at prayer
2400	Hamlet rages at Queen / kills Polonius
2500	Ghost interrupts Hamlet's raging
2600	Queen reports Hamlet's madness
2700	King tells Hamlet he will go to England
2800	Horatio reports Ophelia has lost her mind / Laertes demands his father (Polonius)

Folio 1623

Act-Scene	TLN	Folio 1623 text
I i	100	*Barnardo* . TLN 4 "Who's there?"
I ii	200	*King* . Though yet of Hamlet...
	300	
	400	
I iii	500	*Laer* . My necessaries are...
	600	*Ham* . The Ayre bites shrewdly...
I iv	700	
I v	700	*Ham* . Where wilt thou lead...
	800	
II i	900	*Polon* . Give him his money...
	1000	*King* . Welcome deere Rosen...
II ii	1100	
	1200	
	1300	Hamlet : Denmark's a prison
	1400	Description of child actors

Q2 1604/5

TLN (Q2 column): 3, 100, 179, 200, 300, 400, 462, 500, 600, 604, 682, 700, 800, 890, 900, 1000, 1021, 1100, 1200, 1300, 1400

Bars:
- Horatio discussion of Rome and Julius
- Hamlet soliloquy ... vicious mole of nature

Plot Elements

TLN	Plot Elements
100	Changing of guards at night
	Ghost of old King Hamlet appears to guards
	Concern for activities of young Fortinbras
200	King Claudius assesses threat of Fortinbras
	King instructs ambassadors to Norway
	Laertes requests leave to return to France
	King advises Hamlet on mourning for his father
300	Hamlet laments hasty remarriage of Queen
400	Horatio reports seeing ghost of old King Hamlet
500	Laertes cautions Ophelia about Hamlet
	Polonius gives fatherly advice to Laertes
	Polonius cautions Ophelia about Hamlet
600	Hamlet encounters ghost at midnight
700	Ghost demands revenge for his murder by Claudius
800	Hamlet swears his friends to silence about ghost
	Hamlet plans to put on antic disposition
900	Hamlet laments his role to set things right
	Ophelia reports Hamlet's antic behavior
1000	Polonius concludes that love for Ophelia is cause
	Rosencrantz and Guildenstern arrive
	Polonius reports success of ambassadors
1100	Fortinbras redirected to Poland
	Polonius advises of Hamlet's madness
	Polonius restates that love is cause of madness
1200	Polonius encounters Hamlet's wit
1300	King enlists R & G to spy on Hamlet
	Hamlet discovers R & G were sent for by King
1400	Guildenstern advises of arrival of players
	Hamlet greets players, already known to him

4.4.9

Enter Hamlet, Rosencrans, & c.

Ham.	Good sir whose powers are these?
Cap.	They are of *Norway* sir.
Ham.	How purposd sir I pray you?
Cap.	Against some part of *Poland*.
Ham.	Who commaunds them sir?
Cap.	The Nephew to old *Norway*, *Fortenbrasse*.
Ham.	Goes it against the maine of *Poland* sir,
	Or for some frontire?
Cap.	Truly to speake, and with no addition,
	We goe to gaine a little patch of ground
	That hath in it no profit but the name
	To pay five duckets, five I would not farme it;
	Nor will it yeeld to *Norway* or the *Pole*
	A rancker rate, should it be sold in fee.
Ham.	Why then the *Pollacke* never will defend it.
Cap.	Yes, it is already garisond.
Ham.	Two thousand soules, & twenty thousand duckets
	Will not debate the question of this straw,
	This is th'Impostume of much wealth and peace,
	That inward breakes, and showes no cause without
	Why the man dies. I humbly thanke you sir.
Cap.	God buy you sir.
Ros.	Wil't please you goe my Lord?
Ham.	Ile be with you straight, goe a little before.
	How all occasions doe informe against me,
	And spur my dull revenge. What is a man
	If his chiefe good and market of his time
	Be but to sleepe and feede, a beast, no more:
	Sure he that made us with such large discourse,
	Looking before and after, gave us not
	That capability and godlike reason
	To fust in us unusd, now whether it be
	Bestiall oblivion or some craven scruple
	Of thinking too precisely on th'event,
	A thought which quartered hath but one part wisedome,
	And ever three parts coward, I doe not know
	Why yet I live to say this thing's to doe,
	Sith I have cause, and will, and strength, and meanes
	To doo't; examples grosse as earth exhort me,
	Witnes this Army of such masse and charge,
	Led by a delicate and tender Prince,
	Whose spirit with divine ambition puft,
	Makes mouthes at the invisible event,
	Exposing what is mortall, and unsure,
	To all that fortune, death, and danger dare
	Even for an Egge-shell. Rightly to be great,
	Is not to stirre without great argument,
	But greatly to find quarrell in a straw
	When honour's at the stake, how stand I then
	That have a father kild, a mother staind,
	Excytements of my reason, and my blood,
	And let all sleepe, while to my shame I see
	The iminent death of twenty thousand men,
	That for a fantasie and tricke of fame
	Goe to their graves like beds, fight for a plot
	Whereon the numbers cannot try the cause,
	Which is not tombe enough and continent
	To hide the slaine, o from this time forth
	My thoughts be bloudy, or be nothing worth.

Exit.

4.7.69

	And for his death no wind of blame shall breathe,
	But even his Mother shall uncharge the practice,
	And call it accedent.
Laer.	My Lord I will be rul'd,
	The rather if you could devise it so
	That I might be the organ.
King .	It falls right,
	You have beene talkt of since your travaile much,
	And that in *Hamlets* hearing, for a qualitie
	Wherein they say you shine, your summe of parts
	Did not together plucke such envie from him
	As did that one, and that in my regard
	Of the unworthiest siedge.
Laer.	What part is that my Lord?
King.	A very ribaud in the cap of youth,
	Yet needfull to, for youth no lesse becomes
	The light and carelesse livery that it weares
	Then settled age, his sables and his weedes
	Importing health and gravenes; two months since
	Heere was a gentleman of *Normandy* ,
	I have seene my selfe, and serv'd against the French,

> (Text shown in red above is unique to Q2 vs. F)

4.7.114

King.	*Laertes* was your father deare to you?
	Or are you like the painting of a sorrowe,
	A face without a hart?
Laer.	Why aske you this?
King.	Not that I thinke you did not love your father,
	But that I knowe, love is begunne by time,
	And that I see in passages of proofe,
	Time qualifies the sparke and fire of it,
	There lives within the very flame of love
	A kind of weeke or snufe that will abate it,
	And nothing is at a like goodnes still,
	For goodnes growing to a pleurisie,
	Dies in his owne too much, that we would doe
	We should doe when we would: for this would changes,
	And hath abatements and delayes as many,
	As there are tongues, are hands, are accedents,
	And then this should is like a spend thrifts sigh,
	That hurts by easing; but to the quick of th'ulcer,
	Hamlet comes back, what would you undertake
	To showe your selfe indeede your fathers sonne
	More then in words?
Laer.	To cut his thraot i'th Church.

> (Text shown in red above is unique to Q2 vs. F)

5.2.106

ceedingly my Lord, it is very soultery, as t'were I can-
t tell how: my Lord his Majestie bad me signifie to you, that a
s layed a great wager on your head, sir this is the matter.
eseech you remember.

ay good my Lord for my ease in good faith, sir here is newly
m to Court *Laertes* , believe me an absolute gentlemen, ful of most
cellent differences, of very soft society, and great showing: in-
ede to speake sellingly of him, hee is the card or kalendar of gen-
: for you shall find in him the continent of what part a Gentle-
an would see.

r, his definement suffers no perdition in you, though I
ow to devide him inventorially, would dosie th'arithmaticke of
emory, and yet but yaw neither in respect of his quick saile, but
the veritie of extolment, I take him to be a soule of great article,
his infusion of such dearth and rarenesse, as to make true dixion
him, his semblable is his mirrour, & who els would trace him, his
nbrage, nothing more.

ur Lordship speakes most infallibly of him.
e concernancy sir, why doe we wrap the gentleman in
r more rawer breath?

r.
not possible to understand in another tongue, you will
't sir really.
hat imports the nomination of this gentleman.
Laertes .
s purse is empty already, all's golden words are spent.
him sir.
now you are not ignorant.
vould you did sir, yet in faith if you did, it would not
ich approove me, well sir.
ou are not ignorant of what excellence *Laertes* is.
are not confesse that, least I should compare with
m in excellence, but to know a man wel, were to knowe himselfe.
eane sir for this weapon, but in the imputation laide on
n, by them in his meed, hee's unfellowed.
hat's his weapon?
pier and Dagger.

(Text shown in red above is unique to Q2 vs. F)

5.2.195

Enter a Lord.

Lord, his Majestie commended him to you by young
tricke , who brings backe to him that you attend him in the hall,
sends to know if your pleasure hold to play with *Laertes* , or that
u will take longer time?
m constant to my purposes, they followe the Kings plea-
e, if his fitnes speakes, mine is ready: now or whensoever, pro-
ed I be so able as now.
e King, and Queene, and all are comming downe.
happy time.
e Queene desires you to use some gentle entertainment
Laertes, before you fall to play.
ee well instructs me.
u will loose my Lord.
oe not thinke so, since he went into France, I have bene
continuall practice, I shall winne at the ods; thou would'st not
nke how ill all's heere about my hart, but it is no matter.

(Text shown in red above is unique to Q2 vs. F)

(right column, 2.2)

Ham. In the secret parts
she is a Strumpet.

Rosin. None my Lord; but
honest.

Ham. Then is Doomesday
not true. Let me q
you my good frienc
that she sends you

Guil. Prison, my Lord?

Ham. Denmark's a Prison

Rosin. Then is the World

Ham. A goodly one, in w
fines, Wards, and L
worst.

Rosin. We thinke not so m

Ham. Why then 'tis none
either good or bad,
a prison.

Rosin. Why then your Am
too narrow for you

Ham. O God, I could be
count my selfe a Ki
I have bad dreames

Guil. Which dreames ind
very substance of t
of a Dreame.

Ham. A dreame it selfe is

Rosin. Truely, and I hold
light a quality, that

Ham. Then are our Begge
narchs and out-stre
shall wee to th'Cou
son?

Both. Wee'l wait upon yc

Ham. No such matter. I
rest of my servants:
man: I am most dre
way of friendship,

Rosin. To visit you my Lo

Ham. Begger that I am, I
but I thanke you: an
are too deare a half
your owne inclining
deale justly with m

Guil. What should we sa

(Text shown in red a

s I take it,
reparations
, and the chiefe head
ge in the land.
so;
tentous figure
atch so like the King
of these warres.
indes eye:
state of Rome,
us fell
, and the sheeted dead
e Roman streets
, and dewes of blood
he moist starre,
nes Empire stands,
day with eclipse.
f feare events
ill the fates
omming on
her demonstrated
ntrymen.

m native heere
is a custome
then the observance.
ast and west
of other nations,
with Swinish phrase
ede it takes
ugh perform'd at height
attribute,
er men,
of nature in them
y are not guilty,
his origin)
e complextion
s and forts of reason,
uch ore-leavens
ers, that these men
one defect
tunes starre,
re as grace,
rgoe,
take corruption
e dram of eale
of a doubt

ce defend us:

3.4.72

(Ham.) This was your husband, looke you now what followes
Heere is your husband like a mildewed eare,
Blasting this wholsome brother, have you eyes,
Could you on this faire mountaine leave to feede,
And batten on this Moore; ha, have you eyes?
You cannot call it love, for at your age
The heyday in the blood is tame, it's humble,
And waits uppon the judgement, and what judgement
Would step from this to this, sense sure you have
Els could you not have motion, but sure that sense
Is appoplext, for madnesse would not erre
Nor sense to extasie was nere so thral'd
But it reserv'd some quantity of choise
To serve in such a difference, what devill wast
That thus hath cosund you at hodman blind;
Eyes without feeling, feeling without sight,
Eares without hands, or eyes, smelling sance all,
Or but a sickly part of one true sense
Could not so mope: o shame where is thy blush?

3.4.161

Ger.   O *Hamlet* thou hast cleft my hart in twaine.
Ham. O throwe away the worser part of it,
And leave the purer with the other halfe,
Good night, but goe not to my Uncles bed,
Assume a vertue if you have it not,
That monster custome, who all sence doth eate
Of habits devill, is angell yet in this,
That to the use of actions faire and good,
He likewise gives a frock or Livery
That aptly is put on, to refraine night,
And that shall lend a kind of easines
To the next abstinence, the next more easie:
For use almost can change the stamp of nature,
And either the devil, or throwe him out
With wonderous potency, once more good night,

3.4.203

Ham. I must to *England* , you knowe that.
Ger.   Alack I had forgot.
Tis so concluded on.
Ham. Ther's letters seald, and my two Schoolefellowes,
Whom I will trust as I will Adders fang'd,
They beare the mandat, they must sweep my way
And marshall me to knavery: let it worke,
For tis the sport to have the enginer
Hoist with his owne petar, an't shall goe hard
But I will delve one yard belowe their mines,
And blowe them at the Moone: o tis most sweete
When in one line two crafts directly meete,

Shakespeare's *Hamlet*

The text of the 2nd Quarto (Q2)
vs.
The text of Folio *Hamlet* (F)

There are over 200 lines of dialogue
in Q2 that do not appear in the Folio,
and there are close to 100 lines
in the Folio that do not appear in Q2.

A major portion of these lines,
unique to each text, appear in
the 10 significant blocks of
dialogue unique to Q2 vs. F
and
the three significant blocks of
dialogue unique to F vs. Q2.

These lines of dialogue have been
reproduced in red in the passages
shown on the following two pages.
The lines reproduced in black
are common to Q2 and F.

Not shown are the 21 smaller passages,
ranging from one to three lines each,
as well as the hundreds of
single-word variants.

Reproduced from
The Hamlet 3x2 Text Research Toolset

1.1.108

So by his father lost; and
Is the maine motive of ou
The source of this our wa
Of this post hast and Ron

Bar. I thinke it be no other, bu
Well may it sort that this
Comes armed through ou
That was and is the quest

Hora. A moth it is to trouble th
In the most high and palm
A little ere the mightiest.
The graves stood tennatle
Did squeake and gibber ir
At starres with traines of
Disasters in the sunne; an
Upon whose influence *Ne*
Was sicke almost to doon
And even the like precurs
As harbindgers preceadin
And prologue to the *Ome*
Have heaven and earth to,
Unto our Climatures and
Enter Ghost.

(Text shown in red above

1.4.17

Hora. Is it a custome?
Ham. I marry ist,
But to my minde, though
And to the manner borne,
More honourd in the brea
This heavy headed reveale
Makes us tradust, and taxe
They clip us drunkards, ar
Soyle our addition, and in
From our atchievements, t
The pith and marrow of ou
So oft it chaunces in partic
That for some vicious mol
As in their birth wherein t
(Since nature cannot choos
By their ore-grow'th of so
Oft breaking downe the pa
Or by some habit that too
The forme of plausive mar
Carrying, I say the stamp c
Being Natures livery, or Fe
His vertues els be they as
As infinite as man may un
Shall in the generall censu
From that particuler fault:
Doth all the noble substanc
To his owne scandle.
Enter Ghost.
Hora. Looke my Lord it comes.
Ham. Angels and Ministers of gr

(Text shown in red above i

ortune? Oh, most true:
at's the newes?
t the World's growne

eere: But your newes is
ion more in particular: what have
deserved at the hands of Fortune,
Prison hither?

.
h there are many Con-
geons; *Denmarke* being one o'th'

Lord.
you; for there is nothing
t thinking makes it so: to me it is

ion makes it one: 'tis
inde.
nded in a nutshell, and
of infinite space; were it not that

d are Ambition: for the
Ambitious, is meerely the shadow

ut a shadow.
nbition of so ayry and
is but a shadowes shadow.
bodies; and our Mo-
t Heroes the Beggers Shadowes:
for, by my fey I cannot rea-

ll not sort you with the
or to speake to you like an honest
fully attended; but in the beaten
hat make you at *Elsonower*?
, no other occasion.
n even poore in thankes;
sure deare friends my thanks
ny; were you not sent for? Is it
Is it a free visitation? Come,
come, come; nay speake.
my Lord?

2.2.338

Ham.	How chances it they travaile? their resi-dence both in reputation and profit was better both wayes.
Rosin.	I thinke their Inhibition comes by the meanes of the late Innovation?
Ham.	Doe they hold the same estimation they did when I was in the City? Are they so follow'd?
Rosin.	No indeed, they are not.
Ham.	How comes it? doe they grow rusty?
Rosin.	Nay, their indeavour keepes in the wonted pace; But there is Sir an ayrie of Children, little Yases, that crye out on the top of question; and are most tyrannically clap't for't: these are now the fashion, and so be-ratled the common Stages (so they call them) that many wearing Rapiers, are affraide of Goose-quils, and dare scarse come thither.
Ham.	What are they Children? Who maintains 'em? How are they escoted? Will they pursue the Quality no longer then they can sing? Will they not say afterwards if they should grow them selves to common Players (as it is like most if their meanes are no better) their Writers do them wrong, to make them exclaim against their owne Succession.
Rosin.	Faith there ha's bene much to do on both sides: and the Nation holds it no sinne, to tarre them to Controversie. There was for a while, no mony bid for argument, unlesse the Poet and the Player went to Cuffes in the Question.
Ham.	Is't possible?
Guild.	Oh there ha's beene much throwing about of Braines.
Ham.	Do the Boyes carry it away?
Rosin.	I that they do my Lord, *Hercules* & his load too.
Ham.	It is not strange: for mine Unckle is King of Denmarke, and those that would make mowes at him while my Father lived; give twenty, forty, an hundred Ducates a peece, for his picture in Little. There is some-thing in this more than Naturall, if Philosophie could finde it out.

Flourish for the Players.

Guil.	There are the Players.

5.2.69

Ham.	Does it not, thinkst thee, stand me now upon He that hath kil'd my King, and whor'd my Mother, Popt in betweene th'election and my hopes, Throwne out his Angle for my proper life, And with such coozenage; is't not perfect conscience, To quit him with his arme? And is't not to be damn'd To let this Canker of our nature come In further evill.
Hor.	It must be shortly knowne to him from England What is the issue of the businesse there.
Ham.	It will be short, The interim's mine, and a mans life's no more Then to say one: but I am very sorry good *Horatio*, That to *Laertes* I forgot my selfe; For by the image of my Cause, I see The Portraiture of his; Ile count his favours: But sure the bravery of his griefe did put me Into a Towring passion.
Hor.	Peace, who comes heere?

Enter young Osricke.

Osr.	Your Lordship is right welcome back to Denmarke.